WHATEVER HAPPENED TO...?

Catching Up With Canadian Icons

by Mark Kearney and Randy Ray

A HOUNSLOW BOOK

A MEMBER OF THE DUNDURN GROUP

TORONTO · OXFORD

Editor: Tony Hawke
Copy-editor: Jennifer Gallant
Design: Alison Carr
Printer: Transcontinental

Library and Archives Canada Cataloguing in Publication

Kearney, Mark, 1955-
    Whatever happened to...? : catching up with Canadian icons / Mark Kearney and Randy Ray.

ISBN 10: 1-55002-654-2
ISBN 13: 978-1-55002-654-2

    1. Celebrities--Canada. I. Ray, Randy, 1952- II. Title.

FC25.K42 2006   920.071   C2006-904260-8

1   2   3   4   5   10   09   08   07   06

Conseil des Arts   Canada Council
du Canada   for the Arts

Canadä

ONTARIO ARTS COUNCIL
CONSEIL DES ARTS DE L'ONTARIO

We acknowledge the support of the **Canada Council for the Arts** and the **Ontario Arts Council** for our publishing program. We also acknowledge the financial support of the **Government of Canada** through the **Book Publishing Industry Development Program** and **The Association for the Export of Canadian Books**, and the **Government of Ontario** through the **Ontario Book Publishers Tax Credit program** and the **Ontario Media Development Corporation.**

Care has been taken to trace the ownership of copyright material used in this book. The author and the publisher welcome any information enabling them to rectify any references or credits in subsequent editions.
J. Kirk Howard, President

Printed and bound in Canada
Printed on recycled paper
www.dundurn.com

Cover photos:
Casey and Finnegan: CBC Still Photo Collection
The First Snowmobile: Courtesy of Musée J. Armand Bombardier
Canada Flag: © All rights reserved. Reproduced with the permission of the Canadian Conservation Institute, Department of Canadian Heritage, 2006.
Bob White: Tom Burton – CAW Canada
Manon Rheaume: Hockey Hall of Fame
John McCrae: Courtesy of Guelph Civic Museum, McCrae House
Russ Jackson : Canadian Football Hall of Fame and Museum
Susan Jacks: Courtesy of Susan Jacks

Dundurn Press
3 Church Street, Suite 500
Toronto, Ontario, Canada
M5E 1M2

Gazelle Book Services Limited
White Cross Mills
High Town, Lancaster, England
LA1 4XS

Dundurn Press
2250 Military Road
Tonawanda, NY
U.S.A. 14150

WHATEVER HAPPENED TO...?

WHATEVER HAPPENED TO...?

CONTENTS

• • •

ACKNOWLEDGEMENTS

• • •

FINDING OUT WHATEVER HAPPENED to Canadian icons was a methodical process that required the help of the many people who talked to us, shared vital information, or pointed us in the right direction.

Of course, we want to thank all those featured in our book who graciously took the time to answer our questions, respond to our emails and phone calls, and talk about their lives. We appreciate the information they shared with us.

As always we're grateful to many government officials, public relations and communications professionals, association spokespersons, archivists, and friends and relatives of these icons who gave us the information we needed or told us about people who would. A special thanks to Darlene Martin, Christine McLeod, Ruth Ellen Soles, Rachel Hard, David Monaghan, Garth Wilson, and Arlene McGovern.

We don't have space to name everyone, but we'd like to acknowledge the many journalists and historians who have written about these Canadian icons over the years and left behind terrific information and anecdotes to make our writing task easier.

We owe a big thanks to all our friends at the Professional Writers Association of Canada and Ottawa Independent Writers, and to other writing colleagues, particularly Rosemary Neering, James Reaney, Jaimie Vernon, Mark Shainblum, Bob Pomerantz, Mike Filey, Ian MacLeod, Charles Maginley, Dennis Roddy, and Earl McRae, for helping us dig up contact names, numbers, and facts.

As always, we want to acknowledge the staffs and excellent collections of the Ottawa Public Library, the London Public Library, Library and Archives Canada, and various museums, including the Canada Science and Technology Museum and the Canadian War Museum in Ottawa, the Canadian Warplane Heritage Museum in Hamilton, and the Maritime Museum of the Atlantic in Halifax. Their staffs, while often overwhelmed with work, always found time to answer our questions.

We also want to thank various sports associations and leagues, particularly James Bunton at Canada Sports Hall of Fame and staff at the National Hockey League, the Canadian Football League, the Hockey Hall of Fame, and the Canadian Football Hall of Fame and Museum.

Friends and colleagues who offered ideas, tidbits, and encouragement included John Firth, Ed Janiszewski, Richard Patterson, Doug Ball, Harold Wright, Louise Rachlis, Paul Cassidy, John Einarson, Alan Sainsbury, Liam Maguire, and Carl Dow. An extra salute to the late George Munhall for supportive words to a young would-be writer many years ago. Thank you all.

We must also pass along our gratitude to some newspaper and magazine editors across the land, including those at *Forever Young* in Ottawa, who faithfully published some of these items as we were researching our icons. And a heartfelt thank you goes out to our loyal readers everywhere who have supported our seven previous books and who have visited the Trivia Guys website at www.triviaguys.com.

As always, we appreciate the special attention we have received from the folks at The Dundurn Group in Toronto, particularly Tony Hawke, Kirk Howard, Jennifer Scott, Alison Carr, and Jennifer Gallant. This is our sixth book with Dundurn, and we have always found the staff to be professional and enthusiastic. The occasional free dinners and drinks on their tab are great, too.

Finally, we're ever thankful to our wives, Janis Ray and Catherine Blake, for their support, advice, and ideas about our latest endeavour. It is to Janis and Catherine, the Ray boys, Chris, Andrew, and Marcus, and our faithful home office canine companions, Duffy and the late lamented Watson, whom we dedicate this book.

Randy Ray and Mark Kearney

INTRODUCTION

• • •

KEN TAYLOR, THE CANADIAN AMBASSADOR who rescued a handful of American hostages in Iran. Canada's first self-propelled automobile, long-distance swimmer Marilyn Bell, and labour leader Bob White. The inventor of the Tim Hortons Roll Up the Rim contest, Denny Doherty of the Mamas & the Papas, and the original Maple Leaf flag.

Over the course of Canada's history, these and other people, places, and things have played a significant or interesting role in the development of our country. As a result, some remained in the public eye for an extended period. Others basked in the limelight for as long as an adoring public let them or until they could no longer perform at the level that put them on the national stage in the first place.

Eventually, they faded from our collective consciousness, occasionally popping up as a trivia question or in brief snatches of conversation when talk turns to the good old days.

Whatever happened to these people, places, and things? Where are they now? And what are their stories?

You'll find the answers to these questions and more in *Whatever Happened To...?: Catching Up With Canadian Icons*, which tracks the fate of some one hundred celebrities, newsmakers, and important artifacts from our past.

Over the course of the past year, we've unearthed stories about once-famous musicians, athletes, political figures, and heroes, and we've mixed in fascinating facts and stories about important objects that have left indelible marks on Canadian history.

Long after making headlines or burrowing their way into our hearts and minds, they've travelled different roads or in some cases quietly kept to the same path that vaulted them onto the front pages in the first place.

Whatever Happened To...? scours the country to uncover the fate of those whose fifteen minutes of fame (and more) is over.

Tracking down the subjects in our book was no small feat. It took long hours of research, digging, and tenacity. In their heyday, many were as handy as a phone call to their agents; today many have left this country or slipped into enclaves not easily reached.

But as has been the case with our seven previous books, we relished the search, always looking around one more corner or making that extra phone call to unearth the extra fascinating tidbit that makes the quest all the more worthwhile.

Sometimes we got a lucky break and were handed leads in a recently published newspaper or magazine article. But often our detective work involved dozens of telephone calls and emails. And although the book has a Canadian focus, we talked to people in New York, Florida, Alabama, California, and Washington to get the full story. In one case, we got a call from Australia to flesh out the facts we needed; in another, we found answers in London, England.

At first glance, the content of this book may appear to be somewhat random. Some people, we felt, had to be included because we wondered about their fate and we knew many Canadians would feel the same. Other topics might strike you as a bit more obscure or behind the scenes, but we feel their tantalizing tales had to be told.

Some obvious stories were left out, either because the subjects are still fresh in people's minds or because they are still as prominent as before.

Regardless, we have enjoyed the ride, and we hope you will too.

Whatever Happened To...?: Catching Up With Canadian Icons will reacquaint you with some of your favourites from the past. You'll be surprised to learn what some of them have been doing or where they've ended up.

In keeping with our love of trivia, we've spiced up many of our anecdotes with extra information bites to amaze and delight you. And in an era when the Internet rules, we've added some website addresses to help you find additional details.

We can't include everyone or everything in a single book, but if you want to know the whereabouts of someone or something that didn't make it onto these pages, please visit our website, www.triviaguys.com, and let us know whom you'd like featured if we write a sequel.

Whatever the case, please keep in touch. After all, we don't want you wondering whatever happened to *us*.

PERSONALITIES
• • •
Away from the Spotlight's Glare

• • • Scott Abbott and Chris Haney: Trivial Pursuit Inventors

On December, 15, 1979, while sipping a few beers and playing a game of Scrabble, Scott Abbott and Chris Haney invented Trivial Pursuit, a board game that is probably one of Canada's best-known global cultural exports.

Abbott, a sportswriter with Canadian Press, and Haney, photo editor of the *Montreal Gazette*, were hanging around Haney's kitchen table in Montreal looking for double- and triple-word scores and grumbling about the retail price of the game they were playing.

Forty-five minutes later, they'd dreamed up Trivial Pursuit, which by 2006 had sold more than 90 million copies around the globe.

Today, Abbott and Haney won't say how much they're worth, but a group of about thirty people who took a gamble and bought shares in the upstart game have each earned royalties of $1 million or better.

Not a bad return on an idea that was scoffed at in the beginning by both investors and those in the know in the toy and games industry.

The road to success was a difficult one for Abbott and Haney and their two partners, Chris's brother John and their friend Ed Werner. The game was turned down by a number of major game companies, forcing the four partners to finance and market the game themselves.

While visiting toy fairs in the United States and Canada in 1982, they managed to land only a few hundred orders. A big break came about a year later when a marketing consultant shipped the games to the actors featured in the entertainment questions. Pat Boone, Gregory Peck, and James Mason sent back adoring fan letters, which were used as part of the game's promotional material.

When *Time Magazine* reported that Trivial Pursuit had become popular with the cast of the quintessential boomer flick *The Big Chill*, the game attained a newfound cachet and ushered in the age of trivia.

The rest is part of Canada's trivial lore.

"Let's face it, if we'd called it Quizmaster 6000, it wouldn't have had the same cachet," Abbott told the *Toronto Star* in a 2004 interview. "We were definitely part of the leading edge in this new era of media bombardment."

Exactly what happened once Haney and Abbott attained millionaire status is a question that might make it into their game someday. In 2006, they were living near Caledon, Ontario, a picturesque area about fifty kilometres northwest of Toronto. They built and continue to be majority owners of two golf courses in the rolling hills near their homes — the Devil's Pulpit and the Devil's Paintbrush, which some say are among the best courses in this country.

"Other than that, they are just great friends," says Doug Ball, a former newspaper photographer who has known the pair for more than twenty-five years.

Abbott continues to be an avid sports fan and follows closely the Brampton Battalion, a Junior A team he owns in the Ontario Hockey League. Abbott and John Haney also have interests in the horse racing business. When last contacted, John Haney was living in Toronto. Werner was living in St. Catharines.

Trivial Pursuit made Abbott and Haney, and others, millionaires.

Derrick Ramsey: One of the Lucky Ones

When Scott Abbott and Chris Haney dreamed up Trivial Pursuit in 1979, most of their colleagues and friends figured it was just another of the pair's wacko ideas.

Derrick Ramsey thought otherwise.

Then a twenty-three-year-old clerk in the newsroom library at the *Montreal Gazette*, Ramsey dug into his savings and became one of about thirty people who in the early 1980s invested $1,000 or more in the wildly successful board game.

The quarterly shareholder's cheques he receives each year, "some big, some small, some medium," have paid him about $1 million in royalties over the past twenty-five years.

"The two guys seemed to need money, and I thought they could make a go of it with the game, although a lot of others said 'no way ... they'll just drink the money,'" says Ramsey, now a copy editor in the *Gazette*'s entertainment department.

After listening to Abbott and Haney's pitch in the American Tavern, a popular watering hole once located across the street from the newspaper, Ramsey wrote a cheque for $500 and later cashed in some Canada Savings Bonds to come up with the remaining $500.

"I figured if I got $5,000 back I would be happy," says Ramsey, who believes he is one of two Montrealers who sunk money into Trivial Pursuit.

Evidence that he'd made the right move began to trickle in about two years later, when he received his first cheque for about $500. But the first big payoff came in the mid-1980s when he and his fellow investors attended a shareholders' meeting in Toronto.

Each was handed an envelope; his contained a cheque for $54,000, while others who invested $2,000 received more than $100,000. Shareholders were hooting and hollering with joy. "We were all very surprised, we never expected it."

Thanks to the taxman's bite, Ramsey is not a millionaire, nor is he well off. But the return on his $1,000 investment has paved the way to a fairly comfortable retirement.

His only regret? That he didn't invest $2,000 in the game.

"Had I put that kind of money into the game, I'd probably not be working right now," he says.

• • • John Andrews:
The Man Who Made Us Look Way Up

John Andrews, the key architect behind one of Canada's best-known landmarks, isn't Canadian.

Born in Sydney, Australia, in 1933, Andrews was the main man responsible for designing the CN Tower, the world's tallest free-standing structure, which looms above downtown Toronto. But it's not even his favourite Toronto project (more on that later).

A graduate of the University of Sydney and the Master of Architecture program at Harvard University, Andrews made his way to Toronto, eventually establishing John Andrews Architects in 1962.

Photo by Mark Kearney

The CN Tower was just one of the buildings that made architect John Andrews internationally famous.

Around 1965 he was approached to come up with a design for a metro centre that would have a huge tower as its focal point. Other architects were involved in the project but Andrews was the key player. From the outset it was clear that the tower was to be the tallest in the world, but for Andrews the buildings closer to ground level were just as important.

Interviewed from his home in New South Wales, Australia, Andrews says there were a few different designs for the tower, and the one that stands today is what he calls, perhaps with tongue in cheek, "the lesser of three evils." His design for the CN Tower did call for a revolving restaurant, but it wasn't supposed to have quite the emphasis that it did in the final construction.

Andrews, who has visited Toronto in recent years, says today that "the tower itself is okay" but he wasn't happy with how the structures around it turned out. "It was nice to have done it," he says of the design. "It was a lot of fun." But he says the buildings at the bottom "were a disappointment." Andrews wasn't in Toronto when the 553.33-metre tower was officially opened in 1976.

Andrews recalls that problems with icing near the top of the tower, which was designed to be a communications beacon, were a key challenge. Andrews wanted to consult with the officials of a tall structure in Russia, but he was told that talking to them would be difficult. However, in the end Andrews simply wrote to the engineer there and got a letter back with the details he needed.

Today, the retired architect seems pleased that the tower is something of a Canadian icon and a symbol for Toronto. "But it's not the quality of the bloody Sydney Opera House," for example, he says.

Andrews returned to Australia in 1969 to take on the job of designing the Cameron Offices in Canberra, at that time the biggest office complex of its kind in his native country. He has also made his name designing the Harvard Graduate School of Design (Gund Hall), the American Express Tower in Sydney, and convention centres in Sydney, Melbourne, and Adelaide. In 1980 he was awarded the prestigious Gold Medal from the Royal Australian Institute of Architects for his contribution to architecture, and in the early 1980s he won the competition to design the Intelsat headquarters in Washington, D.C.

Interestingly enough, when asked what his favourite designs in his career are, he has the CN Tower further down the list than another Toronto project. Andrews says designing the first stage of Scarborough College, a part of the University of Toronto campus, is one of his most memorable projects because the job came early in his career.

WORTH NOTING...

The CN Tower's thirty-year reign as the world's tallest free-standing structure may be coming to end. Plans are in place to build a six-hundred-metre tower for Japan's major broadcasting networks in Tokyo. The $420-million tower is scheduled to be completed by 2011.

• • • Ron Buist: He Got Us Rolling Up the Rim

When Ron Buist joined Tim Hortons in 1977 as marketing director, the chain had seventy-nine stores, mostly in Ontario. When he retired twenty-four years later, the company had more than two thousand outlets and was a major presence across Canada and in the northern United States.

Along the way, Buist invented the company's popular Roll Up the Rim to Win promotion, which was introduced on a trial basis in 1986. His goal was to develop an easy-to-play contest that would reward existing customers for their loyalty, attract new customers, and induce all to buy large rather than regular-size cups of coffee, all at the lowest possible cost to store owners.

The promotion was launched after Buist met with Tim Hortons' paper cup supplier in Toronto in 1985 and learned there was room beneath the rim of the cups where a few words could be printed and hidden to describe prizes coffee drinkers could win as part of the promotion.

His initial ideas for the contest name included "Turn Up and Win," which sounded too much like a vegetable; "Roll and Win"; and "Roll Up the Rim and Win." Eventually he decided on "Roll Up the Rim to Win," which he describes as "clear, simple, instructive and entirely honest."

For the first two years, the prizes were limited to Tim Hortons products such as coffee, donuts, muffins, and cookies. Eventually larger prizes such as vehicles, televisions, portable phones, barbecues, and home entertainment systems were added.

In 2005, the company, which is a wholly owned subsidiary of Wendy's International Inc., gave away 30 2005 GMC Canyons, 84 plasma televisions, 460 cash

Bill Booth Photography

Marketing director Ron Buist saw an opportunity under the rim.

prizes of $1,000, 6,644 camping packages, and millions of Tim Hortons food prizes.

Buist, sixty-seven, retired from Tim Hortons in December 2001. The father of two grown children lives in Oakville, Ontario, with his wife, Mary Ann.

In 2003, his book *Tales from Under the Rim* was published by Goose Lane Editions of Fredericton, New Brunswick, and to date has sold more than eight thousand copies. In his spare time, Buist plays golf, writes, travels, and works as a professional speaker.

CBC Still Photo Collection

Casey and Finnegan live in a trunk of their own in British Columbia now that Mr. Dressup is no longer with us. (See story at right.)

• • • Casey and Finnegan: Life after Mr. Dressup

Though most people may hesitate to use the word *beloved* when it comes to puppets, anyone who grew up watching CBC's *Mr. Dressup* might make an exception for Casey and Finnegan.

The two puppets, a boy and a dog, were mainstays on the popular TV program and played an important role in the tales from the Tickle Trunk and life lessons that Ernie Coombs, a.k.a. Mr. Dressup, passed on to generations of children.

But with the end of the show in 1996 and the death of Coombs in 2001, Casey and Finnegan are merely memories for most. Not so for Judith Lawrence, the Australian-born puppeteer and educator who brought Casey and Finnegan to life for some three decades, first on the program *Butternut Square* and more famously on *Mr. Dressup*.

Lawrence not only created these television icons but also provided their voices. With a background in early childhood education and a long love of puppeteering, Lawrence was a natural for children's programming. Now living on an island in British Columbia, Lawrence speaks fondly of the puppets she keeps in a box at her home. She occasionally pulls them out for performances, but for the most part Lawrence has been retired since the 1990s.

There are, in fact, two Finnegans and one Casey residing with Lawrence, and over the years she has had to replace parts of these puppets as they grew old with wear. Lawrence, who likes to maintain her privacy, still occasionally hears from people who were fans of the show and says people recognize her voice from time to time.

AND ANOTHER THING...

Though there is a Casey and a Finnegan in a museum in Ottawa, they are replicas, not originals, Lawrence says.

• • • Richard Comely:
The Man behind Captain Canuck

Though Canada has had several patriotic comic book superheroes over the years, few took off the way Captain Canuck did.

"Born" in 1971 when art student Ron Leishman suggested an idea to Richard Comely, another artist, Captain Canuck came out at a time when feelings of nationalism were high and a gap in the comic book world was there to be filled.

Comely had been a sign painter, crest designer, and fashion and embroidery designer up to that point, but he'd also worked as an illustrator/paste-up artist for a printer while living in Winnipeg. By the time the first Captain Canuck hit the stands in 1975 (Leishman's involvement had dwindled in the preceding years), the idea of a Canadian superhero was still unique. The comic book world was still dominated by American firms Marvel and DC Comics.

That didn't make Comely's job any easier. He published on a shoestring budget and did everything — wrote, drew, coloured, sold ads, and sold comics to dealers. Captain Canuck was a media hit, however. *Time Magazine* featured the new superhero in one of its issues, and in 1980 he made the front page of the *Los Angeles Times*.

A couple of artists joined Comely to help produce the comic book, and operations moved to Alberta. Several issues of Captain Canuck were produced until about 1981, when Comely went on to create issues of *Star Rider and the Peace Machine*. He moved to Cambridge, Ontario, in the mid-1980s, where he became a member of the Director's Guild and did some freelance illustration for TV productions.

He suffered a setback in 1991 when he crashed into a large tree stump, shattering his right elbow, breaking his left wrist, cutting his head open, and badly bruising his ribs and right knee. After several months of recovery, Comely regained complete use of his right arm. In 1992 the National Archives (now known as Library and Archives Canada) acquired all the available original artwork for Captain Canuck from Comely.

The superhero was kept alive in a newspaper strip that ran in eight newspapers in 1995 and 1996 and also appeared as a postage stamp in the mid-1990s.

Despite challenges along the way, Captain Canuck has never quite gone away. A new comic book featuring the superhero was released in summer 2006, the first of what Comely hopes will be several issues annually. In September 2006, Comely began teaching about comic books, storytelling, and comic strips at the Brantford, Ontario, campus of Mohawk College and says he hopes students will help with future Captain Canuck issues. With limited enrollment, Mohawk's new post-graduate Comic Design and Scripting program is the only one of its kind in Canada. "They'll see the whole process from A to Z," Comely said from his Cambridge home. "The involvement by the students will add energy to the whole thing."

Sinking Ship Productions Inc. in Toronto has optioned Captain Canuck for future programs. Comely says the plan will be to start with a half-hour animated series for television and then ultimately a live-action feature film primarily aimed at the Canadian market. He's not sure who might star as Captain Canuck but says Canadian actor Hayden Christensen, who played the young Anakin Skywalker/Darth Vader in the last two *Star Wars* films, might be a good choice.

Courtesy of Richard Comely

Captain Canuck is a fixture in the comic world to this day thanks to creator Richard Comely.

Meanwhile, Comely still hears from fans on a regular basis, many of them Canadians now living in the U.S. who grew up reading the comic. He says it's "a bit strange" to hear from them, but as an artist he likes that fans are still loyal.

• • • Fox Facts:
Artifacts from the Marathon of Hope

On April 12, 1980, Terry Fox left St. John's, Newfoundland, and began running along the Trans-Canada Highway en route to Canada's west coast. The Winnipeg native's goal was to raise money to fight the cancer that had taken his right leg.

Along the way, he captivated the imaginations of thousands of Canadians before learning on December 22, 1980, that his terminal cancer had returned. Fox died on June 28, 1981. By the time his run was cancelled, he had covered 5,373 kilometres, the equivalent of 128 marathons.

Across Canada, Terry Fox Runs held every September keep the memories of Fox alive, as does the millions of dollars raised by the Terry Fox Foundation to fight the killer disease.

Various bits of memorabilia also keep Terry's legacy in the minds of Canadians, says his brother Darrell, who was involved in the run and is national director of the foundation.

The artificial leg, the tattered white sock he wore on that leg, a pair of his running shorts, and one of the twenty-six pairs of shoes he wore during the run, as well as many gifts he received along the way, are on display at the Terry Fox Library in Port Coquitlam, B.C., Terry's hometown.

Courtesy of Darrell Fox

Terry Fox training near his home on Morrill Street in Port Coquitlam, British Columbia, prior to his Marathon of Hope in 1980.

Most of the Marathon of Hope memorabilia that Terry received while on the road or that was forwarded to his father, Rolly, and mother, Betty, is on display or in storage at the British Columbia Sports Hall of Fame in Vancouver. His parents have other more personal belongings, such as Terry's journal.

The home at 3337 Morrill Street in Port Coquitlam where Terry spent his formative years was sold. The van used to accompany Terry on the Marathon of Hope existed in British Columbia's lower mainland only a few years ago, but Darrell has no idea where it is now.

"We are hoping they [the owners] will step forward," he told us in an interview.

• • • Scott Ingram: The Boy in the Bike Commercial

It's arguably one of the most famous TV commercials ever produced in Canada and certainly one of the most award-winning.

Known as "The Bike Story," the commercial, first shown some fifteen years ago, depicted a young boy on a farm wishing for a bicycle he sees in the Canadian Tire catalogue. He clips the picture of it out of the catalogue, much to his father's chagrin, and carries it around. One day his father asks him to help lift some tires out of a truck. The boy reluctantly walks over to do the chore, only to watch as his father lifts out the bicycle he has bought for the son.

It was a simple enough story, but it touched the hearts not only of Canadians but also of other people around the world where it has been shown over many years, winning several awards for excellence in commercials. Canadian Tire used an image from that commercial to celebrate its seventy-fifth anniversary, and the image was later issued as a stamp.

But who were that boy and father and what happened to them after that famous commercial? Singer-songwriter Brent Titcomb starred as the father while Scott Ingram of Richmond, B.C., played the boy. For Ingram, who turned twenty-seven in early 2006, it was one of the first commercials he had ever done. He had appeared in photo shoots before, but the Canadian Tire commercial was his biggest role.

Speaking from British Columbia, where he works as a front desk manager at a hotel, Ingram recalls auditioning for the part and believing he got

Courtesy of Scott Ingram

Scott Ingram, the young boy in the famous Canadian Tire "Bike Story" commercial, as he looks today.

the role because he "had a certain look" the creative team wanted. "I got lucky," he says.

The commercial was shot on a farm outside Toronto, and Ingram has nothing but good memories of the role and of working with Titcomb. "For me it was an experience. I was having fun and seeing where it might go. [I thought] maybe it was a start to a career."

But Ingram says he wasn't serious about acting at the time. While he handled the role well and gained fame from it, he never thought of it as being a big deal when it ran. "I enjoyed shooting it with [Titcomb]. Nothing but good things to say about him. He was fun to be with, a smart, intelligent guy."

Titcomb, too, recalls the commercial fondly, and while he had already carved out a place in Canadian culture with his work in the band 3's A Crowd, and later as a solo folk singer who appeared in countless festivals and concerts across Canada, the Canadian Tire spot certainly got him even more recognized. His audition went well because as soon as he walked into the room "they liked me instantly" and thought he was perfect for the part.

"It was a top-notch production," he says from his Toronto home. "It was one of those things where all the elements came together." He praised the director and production crew for making the work so enjoyable. Titcomb had experience doing voice-overs before he landed this job, but

The famous Canadian Tire "Bike Story" commercial depicted on a Canada Post stamp.

he was reluctant to act in front of the camera at first. Once he got on the set, however, and saw how well he was treated and how professional everyone was, "I thought I'd died and gone to heaven. I thought 'wow,' I'm going to do more of this."

Although both Ingram and Titcomb did other acting jobs after that, both agree the peak experience was "The Bike Story" commercial. Titcomb still does voice-over work and acting jobs when they come along and continues to perform, but he has been busy in the past couple of years with his son Liam's singing career. Liam has made a splash on the charts and in concert while still a teenager.

Ingram, on the other hand, got out of the acting business by the time he hit his teens. "Tons of people" still suggest to him that he get back into acting, and he says he's open to the possibility. For much of his twenties he's worked in the restaurant and hotel business, an area of work he enjoys.

That the commercial did so well was "a big shock," says Ingram, but "I understand how big it is" in viewers' minds. His friends still occasionally introduce him to strangers as the kid in the famous ad, and most of his birthday celebrations involve someone pulling out the commercial to show to partygoers.

But, unlike the boy in the commercial, Ingram didn't get the bike. "No, I didn't get to keep it," he says with a laugh. "Actually, it wasn't too comfortable to ride."

• • • Bruce Kirby: The Legendary Laser

Bruce Kirby has sailing in his blood, so it's no surprise the Ottawa native designed the Laser, one of the world's most popular sailboats.

Kirby began sailing in the Ottawa area as an infant with his father and older brother, David. When he was eight years old, his father designed and built the brothers a twelve-foot, double-ended sloop. It gave the youngsters a boat to use when they were not crewing aboard the family's twenty-four-foot sailboat, the *Velvet*.

By the Second World War the Kirby boys were actively racing a fourteen-foot Peterborough catboat, which had been left to them by a family friend. They soon graduated to the International 14 Class, and by war's end, now teenagers, the brothers were crewing in this hot dinghy class and borrowing boats whenever possible to hone their skills.

After graduating from Ottawa's Lisgar Collegiate in 1949, Bruce joined the *Ottawa Journal* as a reporter and began a career in journalism that lasted until 1975. In the middle of his time at the *Journal* he took a year to sail in Europe with friends aboard a seventy-foot ketch and wrote a series of articles.

Back in Canada, he sailed a Finn in the 1956 Olympics at the age of twenty-seven, a few months after marrying his wife, Margo, and moving to Montreal, where he worked for the *Montreal Star*.

In the fall of 1958, he tried his hand at serious design work with his first International 14, later known as the Kirby Mark I, which was aimed at speed upwind in heavy air. Over the years, Kirby designed a number of variations, all of which were sold internationally.

Courtesy of Margo Kirby

Laser inventor Bruce Kirby lives in Connecticut.

Kirby, his wife, and their daughters, Janice and Kelly, moved in 1965 from Montreal to Chicago, where he became editor of the old *One Design Yachtsman Magazine*, which is now called *Sailing World*.

Six months later, he was asked by a Montreal friend to design a "car topper" dinghy. The result was the Laser, which arrived on the market in January of 1971. The success of this little boat — more than 186,000 have been sold worldwide — inspired Kirby to resign from the magazine and go full-time into sailboat design.

Since then he has come up with about sixty designs, including the twelve-metre *Canada I* and *Canada II*, which were America's Cup challengers in 1983 and 1987. He has also designed several cruising boats, including a line of shallow draft sharpies.

In 1993 the Laser was chosen as one of the Olympic classes and first sailed in the Games in the 1996 event in Savannah. Later, the Laser Radial, which is a Laser with a reduced rig intended for lighter people, was chosen as the women's single-handed Olympic boat.

The Laser is two inches short of fourteen feet in length, is four feet wide, weighs 128 pounds, and has a sail area of seventy-six square feet. It's a one-person boat when racing but can take up to four people for recreational sailing.

A Laser sailboat in action.

Other Kirby designs, the twenty-three-foot Sonar and the Ideal 18, are built by Ontario Yachts in Oakville, Ontario. The Sonar, used for serious racing by Kirby, is also being built in England. Disabled sailors use the Sonar in the Paralympic Games and world championships.

On the racecourse, Kirby competed for Canada in the 1956, 1964, and 1968 Olympic Games. He raced in the Southern Ocean Racing Circuit from 1968 until 1983 and in 1981 was skipper of his own Runaway, a forty-foot fractional sloop that finished fifth in its class and won the Nassau Cup, the final event of the series, in Class C.

Now in his mid-seventies, he lives with his family in the village of Rowayton, Connecticut, on the shores of Long Island Sound, about sixty-five kilometres from New York City, where he runs Bruce Kirby Marine from his home. The family also owns a harbourside home, where he keeps his self-designed thirty-five-foot centre boarder, *Nightwind*.

Kirby continues to designs boats, his most recent being the Pixel, a two-person sailboat for young sailors. He owns the licensing rights to the Laser, with sales of about three thousand units a year. Once built in Pointe Claire, Quebec, it is now produced by boat builders in the United States, England, Australia, Japan, and Chile.

• • • Bill Novinski: Albert! Albert! Albert!

There are many famous hockey players in Canada, but few have warmed people's hearts as much as Albert, the kid in the famous 1980s commercial from Canadian Tire.

Anyone who grew up playing pick-up hockey can relate to the ministory told in the ad. A little kid named Albert is picked last when a bunch of young children are choosing sides for the game. His older brother consoles him, but Albert still feels bad about being the last one chosen. But through persistence and some help from Canadian Tire hockey equipment, Albert at an older age is the star of the team. As he skates onto the ice, the crowd erupts in cheers, shouting his name, and a rival coach says, "I sure wish we had a guy like Albert."

Although the commercial is more than twenty years old, you say the phrase "the Albert Canadian Tire commercial" to people of a certain age and they all nod at the memory. But what about the little kid who played Albert? What became of him? Did he ever excel at the game in real life?

Bill Novinski laughs at the latter question. As a young boy growing up in Long Island, he didn't play hockey. He knew how to skate, but he recalls that he was probably perfectly cast for the role of Albert because he would have been a lousy hockey player. "So it suited me perfectly," he says.

Novinski had done commercials before, but perhaps what gave him an edge at the audition for this one is that he actually knew what Canadian Tire was. Although American, Novinski had relatives in Canada and his family had

Courtesy of Bill Novinski

Albert, played by a young Bill Novinski, was the last player chosen for hockey teams in the famous Canadian Tire commercial.

a summer home in southern Quebec, which meant he was familiar with the outdoor products the famous chain produced. His youthful looks probably helped, too. Although he was about twelve at the time, he had to play Albert as a six- or seven-year-old. "I was very small for my age which helped me get these type parts," Novinski says.

Most of his child acting work until then had been in New York, but the Albert commercial, despite its Canadian flavour, was filmed in Denver, Colorado. "It was a lot of fun," he told us in an interview. "It was a great trip because they really treated us on the set like kings."

Novinski remembers that he had to come up with different emotions when filming the commercial and that it was cold during the shoot. But being from New York he was used to that type of weather. Did he have an inkling that he was filming something that would be so revered by Canadians once it was broadcast?

"I don't think we [he and his mother] knew," he says now. "But we knew it was different in that it wasn't selling a product, it was trying to sell an emotion — the message that if Albert can go on to greater things then anybody can."

Courtesy of Bill Novinski

Once it was broadcast in the mid-1980s, Novinski heard from Canadian relatives that the commercial was getting lots of airtime. But until he was contacted for this book, he said, "I don't know to this day how big it did get up there."

Given that he lived in the U.S., Novinski didn't have people stopping him on the street about the commercial, but a teacher saw a short article in *Sports Illustrated* that mentioned the popularity

Bill Novinski, who lives in Delaware these days, was perfect in the role of young Albert — he was a lousy hockey player.

of the ad in Canada. "It was much bigger than we anticipated," he says.

Novinski continued doing commercial work through college and had a minor role in the 1992 movie *The Light Sleeper*, which starred Susan Sarandon. But he shifted careers as a young adult. These days he's a systems engineer at JP Morgan Chase in Delaware. He's worked there for twelve years and turned thirty-five in 2006. He recalls once having a Canadian co-worker there who was quite impressed to learn that Novinski had played young Albert.

Novinski has two young daughters, and about once a year he still visits the cottage in Quebec. While acting hasn't been a part of his life for several years, he believes he might get back to it if the opportunity ever arises. "I do love acting. That's a part of me."

And while he can't recall just how much he was paid to film the famous commercial, he does remember getting residuals for some time each time it was aired. The pay "was pretty good for kid in the sixth grade," he adds with a laugh.

IN CASE YOU'RE WONDERING...

The young boy who played Albert's brother was Scott Schwartz, who had success as an actor in *The Toy* with Richard Pryor and as the boy who got his tongue stuck on a pole in the seasonal cult favourite *A Christmas Story*. Novinski says the last he heard, Schwartz was in Westwood, California, doing some acting. His name is listed in the credits of a couple of videos made in 2004. The older Albert, who skated onto the ice to the crowd's cheers, was Bill Stewart, who was last known to be living in Colorado. We were unable to reach him.

• • • Joan O'Malley: Canada's Flag Lady

On a snowy Friday night in 1964 — as Canadians eagerly awaited the unveiling of a new flag — Joan O'Malley sewed the first red Maple Leaf flag ever flown.

It was one of three prototypes she helped make for Prime Minister Lester B. Pearson, who by the next day wanted to see what Canada's new flag would look like on a flagpole. Because the job was commissioned after normal business hours, O'Malley's father, Ken Donovan, assistant purchasing director for the Canadian Government Exhibition Commission, was unable to find a seamstress to put the flags together, so he asked Joan to fire up her Singer sewing machine.

On the evening of November 6, O'Malley, then a twenty-year-old secretary at the Indian Affairs Branch of the Department of Citizenship and Immigration, took her machine to the Exhibition Commission's office in south Ottawa, where sometime after midnight she completed the task of hemming the flags. The three designs, which were delivered to the prime minister's residence at 24 Sussex Drive in the middle of the night, included the single red maple leaf on a white background design that became Canada's flag.

Just hours after O'Malley shut down her sewing machine, Pearson raised the Maple Leaf flag at his residence at Harrington Lake in Quebec. The official version of Canada's new flag was flown for the first time in public on February 15, 1965, at Parliament Hill.

After doing her bit for Canada, O'Malley continued to work for the federal government and eventually took a job with the Ontario Attorney General's department in Ottawa. She retired in 1996. She and her husband, Brian, raised two children and now live in south Ottawa.

Canada's lady of the flag lives in Ottawa but spends winters in Florida.

Courtesy of the O'Malley family

The O'Malleys spend time in Panama City Beach, Florida, every winter, where in 2005 and 2006 Joan carried the Canadian flag in an annual ceremony to celebrate Canadian heritage. Back in Canada, Joan occasionally speaks to groups who want to hear the story of how she contributed to the creation of Canada's flag.

One of the early prototypes of the first single-leaf flag, thought to have been sewn by O'Malley, is believed to be at Queen's University in Kingston, Ontario. The whereabouts of the other two versions are unknown.

The sewing machine she used to make the flags is in storage in the couple's basement in Ottawa and may soon be donated to a museum.

Canada's Betsy Ross?

O'Malley's handiwork has occasionally seen her compared to Betsy Ross, the owner of a struggling upholstery business who some say entered U.S. history books in 1776 by sewing America's first flag at the request of General George Washington, who would later become the first president of the United States.

The O'Malleys and others laugh off the notion, saying the Betsy Ross legend is an unconfirmed myth. They point to a February 2005 article in the *Panama City News Herald*, a newspaper that serves the area where they spend their winters:

> When people call Joan O'Malley, creator of Canada's first Maple Leaf flag, "the Canadian Betsy Ross" they are echoing one of America's most persistent myths: the spontaneous creation of America's flag ... the Betsy Ross story came about decades after her death. According to her grandson, Ross had been a friend of George Washington, who asked her to sew the first Stars and Stripes. While it's true that Ross and Washington were friends, that's as true as the story gets. Ross didn't design the flag — Francis Hopkinson, a founding father, was paid for his Stars and Stripes design. While it's fully possible that Ross sewed an American flag at some point, there's no evidence she sewed the first one.

• • • Lea Parrell: The Heinz Baby

In the 1950s and 1960s Lea Parrell (née Jago) was the face of Heinz baby food.

Before she was one year old, a photograph of Parrell with her captivating smile and thick blond hair graced the labels on containers of the Heinz baby food that was spooned into the mouths of babes across Canada and as far away as Europe and Australia.

Parrell, who was raised in Toronto's Beach neighbourhood, was signed as Heinz's baby food poster child before she was born.

The food company's marketing team had their eye on Parrell's four-year-old sister, Syme, a regular on *Cannonball*, a popular CBC-TV series, but decided she was too old. So they approached Syme's pregnant mother, Nancy, and signed up her baby-to-be, who arrived a few months later in November 1958.

Between 1959, when she was four months old, and the late 1960s, Lea's face was on millions of bottles of the baby food. She also hawked the stuff in print advertisements and television commercials. Her memories of the TV work and photo shoots are vague but one incident hasn't faded.

Courtesy of Syme Jago

Lea Parrell in 2006.

"I remember sitting in a high chair … the director wanted me to not like another company's baby food and he wanted me to turn it upside down and dump it on the floor. The director was under the chair. I threw the food on top of his head … everyone thought it was hilarious."

Lea's face was on the baby food containers for about ten years, cutting a profile that helped open the door to other television work as a youngster. By age twelve, she had appeared in 125 TV commercials for products such as Bayer Aspirin, Spoon Size Shredded Wheat, Colgate, Chapstick, and the Eaton's Santa Claus Parade. In 1963, her sister Syme played the role of Gaby La Roche on the CBC-TV show *The Forest Rangers* and had a role in the Disney movie *The Incredible Journey*.

The money the pair earned from television, movies, and commercials was socked away by their parents, Nancy and Ernie Jago, to cover dance, acting, and singing classes and, later, university tuition and textbooks.

After living in Ottawa for four years, Lea returned to Toronto to study commerce and finance at the University of Toronto but found it wasn't for her. She returned to show business, where she was a headline performer in musicals that toured North America, including *A Chorus Line*, *The Cole Porter Musical Review*, *You're the Top*, and *Durante*. She appeared in various television series and worked as a dancer and singer on shows such as a Johnny Cash special and the long-running television show *Circus*.

In 1989, now married to Vince Parrell, a Toronto dancer/producer, and with a daughter, Victoria, part of the family and a second daughter, Deanna, on the way, she decided to slow down. Lea was in the middle of a North American tour and returned to Toronto from San Francisco on October 17, 1989 — the day a devastating earthquake struck. She felt this was a sign for her to move on to another area of show business. At first, she worked as a freelance producer, mainly for large companies; soon

Courtesy of Lea Parrell

Lea Parrell as she appeared on thousands of baby food bottles in the late 1950s and the 1960s.

after she began working as a volunteer for Special Olympics Canada, which is devoted to enriching the lives of Canadians with intellectual disabilities through sport.

"I gave some thought to the blessings I'd enjoyed and decided it was time to give something back," she says. Her initial work with Special Olympics involved helping stage the organization's annual Sport Celebrities Festival. In 1991, she was hired as executive director of the festival, which includes an annual day of events such as a breakfast for 1,400 people, a black-tie dinner, entertainment, and an auction broadcast on TSN.

Lea, forty-eight, lives in Toronto with her husband and until June 2006 was vice-president of marketing and development for Special Olympics Canada. She was a key player in helping the organization raise more than $15 million a year to provide sports programs for athletes with Down's syndrome, autism, and fetal alcohol syndrome and to stage events such as the World Summer and Winter Games and National and Provincial Summer and Winter Games.

In the fall of 2006 she was working for herself in corporate relations, sponsorship sales, and television production and was looking for new challenges.

Syme Jago worked for the Special Olympics Canada Foundation for five years and now works with her husband's Toronto-based lighting design business.

Lea has fond memories of her lengthy career with Special Olympics Canada: "To give athletes that are extremely capable the opportunity to enrich their lives and the lives of their families is extremely motivating."

• • • Hart Pomerantz: Legal and Laughing

He was known as the funny one, but it was his partner Lorne Michaels who went on to become the doyen of North American TV and film comedy. He furthered his reputation as a quick ad libber on a 1970s CBC game show, but the thought of performing alone in front of people gives him stage fright. He wrote for such comedians as Joan Rivers and Phyllis Diller and was a writer on *Laugh-In*, but he seems content to have been a practising lawyer for the past thirty years.

Hart Pomerantz solidified his presence in the Canadian consciousness with his CBC show with Michaels, *The Hart and Lorne Terrific Hour*, as a panellist on *This Is the Law*, and more recently as the host of a short-lived series called *Grumps*. Even today as he works in his solo legal practice helping people who have lost their jobs, he gets stopped by many saying "Hey, aren't you the guy…?"

The soft-spoken comedian-lawyer laughs and says, "The older I get the more famous I am," even though he's been out of the spotlight for much of the past twenty years. But he's never left comedy. In addition to writing many humorous short stories over the years, Pomerantz, who lives in North York, Ontario, says he has a movie script in the works and plenty of ideas for a television comedy. He also enjoys sculpting, photography, inventing — "anything creative interests me."

Despite his stage fright, he's created a monologue of his life that he's performed at synagogues. "It's not that hard to get on stage until you realize you're alone and they're expecting things. You have to be a tough person" to suffer rejection if the audience doesn't like what you do, Pomerantz says.

He wanted to be a comedian ever since he was a child but didn't really know how. He met up with Michaels in the 1960s, when the latter was working on a University of Toronto production called the *Follies* and Pomerantz was trying to get a role in it for his brother. It was Michaels who later contacted him about teaming up, and the two had their first success writing for CBC radio and other comedians.

Their big American break came with an offer to write for a new sitcom starring Phyllis Diller, but the show failed to attract audiences and was cancelled within a few weeks of its debut. In fact, Pomerantz says neither he nor Michaels was told that the show was cancelled and kept showing up for work. Pomerantz ran into some staffers for *Rowan and Martin's Laugh-In*, and the two were signed on as junior writers on what was then the most popular show in America.

The relationship didn't last long. Pomerantz and Michaels were lured back to Canada by the CBC with the promise of their own show and creative control. "We were the bosses instead of the kids," Pomerantz explains.

The *Hart and Lorne Terrific Hour* delighted audiences in the early 1970s, and Pomerantz speaks proudly of it being groundbreaking in blending comedy and rock music together, something that Michaels pioneered in the U.S. on *Saturday Night Live* when it debuted in 1975. As for the breakup between the two, Pomerantz shrugs it off: Michaels wanted to be more of a producer and Pomerantz enjoyed the performing side. And while Michaels's move led to his becoming a comedy icon in North America, Pomerantz enjoyed his own particular limelight and practising law.

"Comedy is for kids and law is for adults. I have ambivalence towards what I want to be. People in show business tend to be childlike in a way. They make it look like a business but it isn't."

Nevertheless, Pomerantz's sharp wit was showcased on *This Is the Law* for several years, while he kept his hand in a legal practice. For fifteen years he practised criminal law but found he wanted the judge to sentence his clients to more time in prison. He shifted to the kind of law that helps people with employment troubles so that he could "do some good in the world."

Comedy still remains a love for him, however, and while he says that "comedians in general are odd people" he admires the work of Chris Rock, Bill Maher, and Woody Allen — "he was the best for me."

Pomerantz has talked to Michaels on occasion over the past twenty years, but "he's gone his way and I chose my route." Meanwhile, Pomerantz seems content with life and is bubbling with enough ideas in different artistic fields to keep him busy.

"Being funny is my favourite thing. I do it every day; it's like breathing."

• • • Ken Taylor:
Ambassador of the Canadian Caper

In 1980, an event known far and wide as "the Canadian Caper" made curly-haired Canadian diplomat Ken Taylor a household name in Canada and around the globe.

In 1979, two decades into a lengthy civil service career that began when he joined the federal government, the native of Calgary was Canada's ambassador to Iran. On November 4 of that year, a band of Iranian revolutionaries invaded the United States Embassy after they suspected the Americans of aiding the Shah of Iran, who had been driven from office by the Ayatollah Khomeini.

During the riot, sixty-six Americans were taken hostage, but six others escaped and hid for four days before reaching the Canadian Embassy.

Two of the fugitives lived with Taylor and his wife, Patricia, in the ambassador's home; four took up residence with immigration officer John Sheardown and his wife, Zena. The remaining American hostages were held by revolutionaries who sought the return of the Shah, who was in a New York hospital.

On January 28, 1980, after the six had been in hiding for nearly three months, the escape began to unfold. Tehran's Mehrabad Airport was carefully scouted; Canadian passports and identity documents were arranged for the Americans; and Canadian Embassy staff, in small groups, quietly returned home.

Canada's American guests navigated their way nervously through the airport and onto an early morning flight to Frankfurt. Later that day, Taylor and the remaining Canadians shut the Embassy down and left Iran.

News of his heroics made Taylor an instant celebrity. He received the U.S. Congressional Gold Medal and thousands of gifts in a ten-month orgy of gratitude. He was portrayed by legendary Canadian actor Gordon Pinsent in the movie *Escape from Iran: The Canadian Caper*.

The American hostages were released in January 1981, on the last day of U.S. President Jimmy Carter's term in office. In 1998 it was revealed that the CIA had planned the Taylor-led escape.

Since the events in Iran, life has been much calmer for Taylor, who turned seventy-two in 2006. He was Canadian Consul General in New

York from 1981 to 1984 and then left the public service, remaining in the U.S. as a senior executive with Nabisco Brands. From 1984 to 1987, he was the company's senior vice-president, government affairs; from 1987 until 1989 he was senior vice-president of RJR Nabisco Inc.

He was made an Officer of the Order of Canada in 1980 and has won numerous other awards, including the Harry S. Truman Good Neighbor Award and the State of California Medal of Merit.

Taylor has served as a board member of a range of companies in Canada, the United States, and Mexico, including Hydro One in Toronto. For more than six years he served as the chancellor of Victoria University in Toronto, which is composed of Victoria College, an arts and science college of the University of Toronto, and Emmanuel College, a theological college of the United Church of Canada.

In 2006, Taylor was living in New York City with his wife, Patricia, a scientist at the New York Blood Center. He is chairman of Taylor & Ryan Inc., which provides counselling services to clients on issues of political risk, international marketing, and strategic accommodation with government.

Courtesy of Ken Taylor

He visits Toronto about forty times a year, mainly to tend to the business of the boards he sits on. He is booked for public speaking engagements about once a month, where, inevitably, he is questioned about his involvement in the Canadian caper.

"Iran is a distant memory, for me," he said in an interview from New York City. "I'm still quizzed about it because it was an incident of some significance at the time.

Ken Taylor rescued American hostages in Iran. He now lives in New York City.

But life goes on … my interests now are what is happening there today versus thinking back to the old days."

• • • Bob White: A Love Affair with Labour

As a young boy growing up in Woodstock, Ontario, in the early 1950s, Bob White received some sage advice from his father: "Whatever you do, don't get involved in the union … they're all a bunch of Communists."

White dismissed his father's words of wisdom and went on to become one of the most influential figures in the Canadian labour movement, respected by workers and business leaders alike and a major voice in national affairs.

His father, Robert, who at the time worked in the same wood factory where Bob and his brother Bill were employed, later became a great supporter of White's work as a trade unionist.

"He told me he understood the importance of trade unions, not only at the workplace but in society in general. He said if anyone criticized me, he would jump to my defence immediately."

White was born in Ballymoney, Northern Ireland, on April 28, 1935, and moved with his family to Canada at age fourteen, eventually settling on

Tom Burton – CAW Canada

a dairy farm near Woodstock. After dropping out of elementary school, he joined Hay and Company, which turned raw logs into plywood and wood used to make furniture.

By age sixteen he was a member of the United Auto Workers union, and within two years he was elected to the post of shop steward at the wood factory. By 1959 he was president of UAW Local 636 and in 1960 was appointed UAW international representative and assigned to organizing duties in Canada.

Bob White pulled Canadians out of the United Auto Workers union to form the Canadian Auto Workers union in 1984.

In 1972, he became administrative assistant to the UAW

director for Canada, Dennis McDermott. Six years later, White was elected UAW director for Canada.

In 1976, he travelled across Canada to mobilize workers for the October 14 Day of Protest against the federal government's wage controls. He also played a key role in the November 21, 1981, protest against interest rates in Ottawa and spearheaded the union's campaign against corporate concession demands, culminating in a five-week strike at Chrysler Canada in November 1982, which started Chrysler workers back to parity with GM and Ford.

In 1984, White was at the centre of one of the most dramatic moments in Canadian labour history when UAW was restructured and the Canadian Auto Workers union (CAW) emerged to reshape the Canadian labour landscape. The founding convention for the new union took place in 1985, and White was acclaimed the first CAW-Canada president and served three terms.

White was elected president of the Canadian Labour Congress (CLC) in June 1992 and was re-elected in 1994 and 1996. During his seven years as CLC president, he was committed to equality and equity issues both inside and outside the labour movement. While president he helped the organization become more representative of Canadian workers by adding Teamsters Canada, teachers, nurses, and most of the building and construction trades to its membership rolls.

Known as a dynamic speaker, talented organizer, and savvy bargainer, he has spoken out in Canada and around the world for human rights and led innovative bargaining for indexed pensions and many other issues. White became a household name during the debates around the Canada–U.S. Free Trade Agreement as one of the most outspoken opponents of the deal.

He was the first major leader in Canada to speak out against cruise missile testing. In Munich, Germany, he put the case before Chancellor Helmut Kohl to put a dramatic rise in OECD-country unemployment on the G7 Summit agenda.

Since retiring as CLC president in 1999, White has continued to do what he does best, speaking out on behalf of workers in Canada, "never forgetting where I came from. Whether I'm speaking to a meeting in Geneva or meeting with world leaders, my thoughts always return to those affected by major issues, the workers.

"When I'm looking at an issue like the economy or globalization or plant closure, I always think of what will happen to families."

In 2006, White and another retired CAW staff member reviewed Canadian Auto Workers' education programs to determine if they were relevant for the future; he was also part of a CAW delegation that attended International Metalworkers Union conferences and was a member of the CAW Social Justice Fund Board, which distributes money for use in a variety of projects such as the elimination of land mines, development of water supplies, and disaster aid.

He was also co-chair of a labour and business advisory committee to the federal labour minister on international labour affairs and in that capacity participated in the 2005 Conference of the Labour Ministers of the Americas in Mexico City.

He continues to sit in on CAW board meetings and often speaks publicly about the labour movement. He has been awarded doctor of law degrees from York University, the University of Windsor, the University of Toronto, St. Francis Xavier University, and the University of Western Ontario. He was made an Officer of the Order of Canada in 1990 for his exceptional service to the country and in 1987 wrote his autobiography, *Hard Bargains: My Life on the Line.*

Looking back, White says his biggest accomplishment was pulling Canadians out of the UAW to form CAW. "Had we stayed with the UAW, we'd be in a union today that would probably at best represent 110,000 members. By going the way we did, we now have 240,000 people … it gave us a better profile in the country and CAW plays a bigger role in the international labour movement than UAW…. In my time, it was the biggest decision we ever made."

White and his wife, Marilyn, a staff member with the Canadian Union of Public Employees, live in Toronto.

• • • Roger Woodward: Falls Survivor

In the summer of 1960, Roger Woodward was at the centre of what the history books have recorded as the "Niagara Falls miracle."

On the afternoon of July 9, the seven-year-old Niagara Falls, New York, youngster and his seventeen-year-old sister, Deanne, were enjoying their first-ever boat ride in an aluminum fishing boat piloted on the Niagara River by family friend Jim Honeycutt.

While cruising above Canada's Horseshoe Falls, the twelve-foot craft's 7.5-horsepower outboard motor hit a rock, sheared its cotter pin, and lost power. As it was swept toward the falls, it capsized, tossing Honeycutt and the Woodward children into the frothing waters.

Roger was wearing nothing but a swimsuit and a life jacket as he floated toward the brink of the falls, which drop 162 feet into a pile of rocks. His sister managed to slip into a life jacket before the boat flipped.

John Hayes and John Quattrochi, both tourists, pulled Deanne out of the water twenty feet from the top of the of Canadian falls but Roger was not so lucky. He went over the edge into an area strewn with boulders.

Miraculously, he escaped with nothing more than minor cuts and bruises, suffered when he landed at the bottom, and a concussion, which happened before he went over the brink.

To this day, Woodward, now in his early fifties, has vivid memories of his experience. "One minute I was looking over the gorge, then I was floating in a cloud, I couldn't see anything. I could not discern up or down or where I was," he says. "What I remember next is a severe throbbing in my head, likely from the concussion, which happened in the rapids or when I fell out of the boat. ... I had surrendered to the fact that I was going to die."

Courtesy of Roger Woodward

Roger Woodward more than forty years after he survived a plunge over Niagara Falls in 1960.

Why did he not perish like others who have gone over the falls?

"There were not a whole lot of places to land but by the grace of God, I landed in a pool of water. Had I even grazed one rock on the way down it would have shattered every bone in my body."

The fifty-five-pound boy was pulled from the river by the crew of a *Maid of the Mist* tour boat, which luckily was cruising nearby with a load of tourists who were snapping photographs of the falls. Roger immediately asked about the whereabouts of his sister and then requested a glass of water.

"I had probably drank half the Niagara River, but I was pretty thirsty," he says.

Back on shore, he was taken to the Greater Niagara General Hospital in Niagara Falls, Ontario, where he remained for three days for treatment of his injuries.

Deanne, with only a cut hand, was treated at a hospital in Niagara Falls, New York, where she learned of her brother's fate. The body of Honeycutt, who also went over the falls, was found in the river four days later. He was not wearing a life jacket.

When the world learned that Woodward had become the first person to go over the falls unprotected, the media descended on the boy and his family. Newspapers took his picture. Movie producers wanted his story.

"The story became famous," he recalls. "It was a time when the daredevil thing and going over the falls was pretty amazing and here you had two kids from a blue collar family who ended up in a horrific accident and a man was killed ... the fact that we lived when many others had died going over the falls was quite amazing."

In 1962, the Woodward family moved to Florida, in part to escape the prying eyes of the media. The parents never talked about the incident with Roger and Deanne. In Florida, Roger met and married his high school sweetheart, Susan. After college he joined the Navy and later worked for a business and office products company in Atlanta for thirteen years before a career change took the family to Michigan, where he worked in the telecom industry for seventeen years.

In 1996, the Woodwards and their three sons moved to Huntsville, Alabama, a city of 350,000 people about 290 kilometres northwest of

Atlanta, where Roger was working in real estate. In 2006, Deanne was living in Lakeland, Florida.

Roger Woodward has returned to Niagara Falls, Ontario, several times since the accident. On the twenty-fifth anniversary in 1985 he and all of those involved in the mishap, including Deanne, were given a key to the city and a portrait of the falls.

Five years later, he spoke to the congregation at Glengate Alliance Church in Niagara Falls, Ontario. The audience was silent as Woodward, thirty-seven years old at the time, told how Honeycutt's boat was caught in the fast-flowing current and dragged toward the edge of the falls.

In 1994 Woodward and Deanne returned to the city to retell their story on a half-hour Canadian television special. Joining Roger and his sister were the two men, in their eighties at the time, who rescued Deanne before she went over the falls.

WORTH NOTING...

The incident at Horseshoe Falls was not Roger Woodward's only brush with death. In his junior year of high school in 1970, a tractor-trailer ran a red light and broadsided his motorcycle. He landed on a set of railroad tracks, escaping with only a broken finger on his left hand.

In the fall of 1994, while on a nighttime boat trip across Lake Huron with his nine-year-old son, Jonathan, the pair became disoriented in a fog bank. Their boat was narrowly missed by a freighter.

The boating incident "was the single most frightening experience since Niagara Falls," says Woodward.

• • • Elwy Yost: Still a Movie Buff

The man who has had a lifelong love affair with movies and spread that joy every Saturday night on TVOntario is still a film fan.

Elwy Yost, host of TVOntario's *Saturday Night at the Movies* for more than twenty years, speaks enthusiastically about movies from his home in West Vancouver, where he has lived since 1988. He talks about seeing the original *King Kong* from the 1930s when he was an eight-year-old boy in Toronto, but also mentions recently seeing the 2005 remake. "We loved it," he said in an interview.

Although he is no longer seen on the popular TV show, it still bears his stamp, as many of the interviews broadcast are from his time on the program. Yost didn't interview everyone who had a role in Hollywood over the past sixty years or so; it just seems that way. During his TVO days, Yost explored themes in movies and journeyed to Hollywood to talk to the actors, writers, directors, cinematographers, and makeup artisans who created memorable movie magic.

Yost could sometimes be overly enthusiastic in his praise of films, but his show distinguished itself by often focusing on the behind-the-scenes people of Hollywood. In fact, that approach helps explain why TVO provided hundreds of interview segments to the Academy of Motion Picture Arts and Sciences for its archives.

Through it all, the affable Yost (or perhaps it's better to refer to him as Elwy as most of his fans seemed to do) never lost the feeling of that eight-year-old boy in his neighbourhood theatre. "Oh, sure I do," he once said in an interview when asked if he still got excited to meet such actors as Jimmy Stewart and Henry Fonda, writers, and directors responsible for some of his favourite flicks. "I'm still a child. I've never grown up. The question 'what is Hollywood?' is hard to answer. It still haunts me."

When Yost began *Saturday Night at the Movies*, he'd already had several years of television experience, notably as a panellist on the game show *Flashback* and as host of *Passport to Adventure*, which was something of a precursor to what *Saturday Night* and his through-the-week program *Magic Shadows* would become. TVO wanted an educational element to its program, and Yost had experience as a teacher. He joked that he was hired as host because his ability to do three jobs as host/writer/producer would save TVO money. The first series of shows in March 1974 was "Three Films in Search of God," in which Yost screened Ingmar Bergman films and invited academics and religious leaders on for discussion.

Before he retired from the show, Yost had spent time writing a novel. The book, *White Shadows: A Novel of Espionage and Adventure*, was published in 2004 and involves romance, adventure, and a lost film that offers a key to one of the best-kept secrets of the twentieth century. "It's quite sexy in places," he says.

These days, having turned eighty, Yost takes it easy. He had a serious operation about a year ago but came through it successfully. Movies are still a big part of his entertainment, which he watches with wife, Lila. "I'm enjoying life; I suppose that's a good way to put it."

WORTH NOTING...

Yost isn't the only successful professional in the family. Son Graham wrote the screenplays for *Speed* and *Broken Arrow*, among others, as well as for the TV series *Boomtown* and *Band of Brothers*.

Photo by Mark Kearney

Elwy Yost was Mr. *Saturday Night at the Movies* for more than two decades at TVOntario.

HISTORICAL ITEMS
• • •
Remembrance of Things Past

• • • Alouette I and II: Spaced Out

With the launch of the Alouette I satellite on September 29, 1962, Canada officially joined the space race. And while Alouette I had to be sent into space from California, it was the first satellite built entirely by a country other than the U.S. or the U.S.S.R.

Canadians were justifiably proud of their satellite, which made Canada the third country in the world to have such an object orbiting the earth. The Soviets had gotten a head start in the world when they launched Sputnik in October 1957. Within a year, North American scientists and politicians, convinced that we were in the age of satellites and concerned about tensions from the Cold War, sought proposals from Canada for experiments in these space objects.

Supporters of this plan believed that a new program should develop Canadian space capability, acquire new data for the engineering of high-frequency radio communication links, and acquire a better understanding of the properties of the ionosphere for scattering and deflecting radar beams.

In those early days, satellites were generally not expected to last more than a few months after their launch, but Alouette I proved to be a hardy piece of machinery. It continued to function and transfer data for ten years before its signal was turned off from the ground. In the meantime, a second satellite, Alouette II, was launched in 1965, and two other satellites were added in 1969 and 1971. Alouette II would also send information for ten years.

Canadian space researchers focused on the earth's upper atmosphere and the ionosphere so that they could better understand radio communication in the far north. Thanks to the work of the two Alouettes, scientists realized that a satellite communications system would be the best way to provide communications for all of Canada. The success of the Alouette satellites led to Canada's reputation as a leader in satellite communications, and in 1987, the Engineering Centennial Board Inc. recognized Alouette as one of the ten most outstanding achievements of Canadian engineering over the last century.

It's been more than three decades since Alouette II stopped sending data. What happened to it and its sister, Alouette I? According to information from the Manitoba Museum, they are both still in orbit, despite their retirement as signal devices. In fact, they are in such high orbits that it will take thousands of years for them to decay; then they'll burn up when they re-enter earth's atmosphere. Alouette I is orbiting the earth about one thousand kilometres high, while Alouette II, which follows a more oval-shaped path, moves in the sky anywhere from five hundred to two thousand kilometres above the planet's surface.

According to a Manitoba Museum scientist, these high orbits mean the satellites are "pretty faint," so the only way to see them pass overhead is to have binoculars and information on exactly where to look. Many other satellites, on the other hand, are visible to the naked eye, and several pass above us each night.

• • • Canadarm: A Canadian Innovation in Space

"Okay, the arm is out for the first time … working great … it's a remarkable flying machine and it's doing exactly as we hoped and expected."

On November 13, 1981, these comments by Space Shuttle Columbia commander Joe Engle and pilot Richard Truly introduced the world to Canadarm, one of Canada's most significant technological achievements in space.

Formally known as the Shuttle Remote Manipulator System, the 15.2-metre arm is the first robotic manipulator system designed for specific use in the harsh environment of space. It is used for positioning astronauts, maintaining equipment, moving cargo, and deploying, capturing, and repairing satellites.

Between 1981 and 1985, five versions of the arm were built in the Toronto factory of Spar Aerospace of Toronto, which later sold its robotics division to MacDonald, Dettwiler and Associates (MDA). The cost of the first Canadarm was $108 million.

Canadarm functions like a human arm. It has six joints: two at its shoulder, one at its elbow, and three at its wrist. The arm emblazoned on its upper boom with the word *Canada* and a Canadian flag is most visible; the system also includes astronaut controls inside the shuttle.

The arm has demonstrated its reliability, usefulness, and versatility through seventy-one flawless missions to date.

Its tasks have been many and varied: over the years, the Canadarm has deployed satellites into their proper orbit and retrieved malfunctioning ones for repair. Beginning with Mission STS-88 in December 1998, the arm has been used in seventeen Space Station assembly missions to install new elements on the station and to support space walks by space construction workers.

Tasks it has performed successfully include loosening a jammed solar array panel and using its elbow and wrist joint cameras for visual inspection of the orbiter and payload. It has also knocked ice off the shuttle's wastewater dumping vents.

Its most notable mission to date occurred in December 1993, with the first servicing of the Hubble Space Telescope. Astronauts used the Canadarm as a mobile work platform to stand on during five space walks required to repair the $1.5-billion astronomy satellite in orbit. The Canadarm played a critical role in retrieving the telescope, placing it in the shuttle Endeavor's cargo bay for repairs, and releasing it in space afterwards, says the Canadian Space Agency.

"The Canadarm is our nation's most recognized science achievement. It is the icon of Canadian scientific know-how," says the agency.

The development of Canadarm began in the early 1970s, when the National Aeronautics and Space Administration (NASA) was looking for international partners to contribute to its novel Space Transportation System, better known as the Space Shuttle.

The government of Canada, through the National Research Council, invested $108 million in designing, building, and testing the first Canadarm flight hardware, unit 201, which was Canada's contribution to NASA's manned space flight program for the orbiter Columbia. In return, NASA contracted to buy at least three more robotic arms, units 301 and 302 in 1983 and unit 303 in 1985.

MDA designed and built each of the 410-kilogram robotic arms, which have nerves of copper wiring, bones of graphite fibre reinforced tubing, and muscles of electric motors, all controlled by a sophisticated computer, the brains of the system, which also provides essential guidance information to the astronauts who use it, including Canadians Chris Hadfield and Mark Garneau.

In place of a hand, the Canadarm has a cylindrical end effector, a wire-snare device that fits over a special prong, or grapple fixture, attached to the payload that it handles. Inside the shuttle flight deck, astronauts at the SRMS station use two hand controllers to operate the Canadarm either one joint at a time or with all six joints moving in a coordinated manner.

Since 1981, the four arms have undergone numerous hardware changes, improvements in manufacturing processes, and control software alterations.

The Canadarm technology has generated spin-offs in areas other than space. The technology has found applications in remote manipulators designed to extend human dexterity into hostile environments and medical applications.

Canadians wanting to get up close and personal with the

Canadarms that have travelled into space are out of luck.

The third Canadarm, known as Canadarm S/N 302, was lost on the Challenger Mission 51L when the shuttle blew up above the Atlantic Ocean seventy-three seconds after takeoff from Cape Canaveral, Florida, on January 28, 1986. Along with a large piece of Challenger, remnants of Canadarm S/N 302 are buried in a former missile silo near the Kennedy Space Center at Cape Canaveral, says NASA spokesperson Allard Beutel.

That arm was replaced in the Canadarm inventory with unit 202 in 1993. Arm 202 and three others — Arm 201, the original unit; Arm 301, the second unit; and Arm 303, the fourth unit — are usually kept at Cape Canaveral for use on space shuttle missions but occasionally are sent to MDA's Brampton, Ontario, factory for testing and updating, says Jim Middleton, vice-president of strategic business development of MDA, who was the chief engineer in charge of building the first Canadarm.

Courtesy of NASA

Canadarm: a great Canadian innovation.

Full-size inoperable models of the Canadarm are on display at the Canada Science and Technology Museum in Ottawa and the Ontario Science Centre in Toronto.

For more information, visit www.sciencetech.technomuses.ca, www.ontariosciencecentre.ca, and www.mdacorporation.com/space-missions.

• • • Canada's Constitution: The Original Is Still Overseas

Canada's constitution, formally known as *The British North America Act, 1867*, was patriated in 1982, but you won't find the document in Canada.

The BNA Act was a law enacted by the British Parliament but largely drafted by Canada's Fathers of Confederation beginning at the momentous Charlottetown Conference of 1864, which led to the birth of Canada in 1867.

Although the Act has been under Canadian control since a historic April 17, 1982, ceremony at Parliament Hill brought into force *The Constitution Act, 1982*, the original BNA Act has never been brought home to Canada.

It sits in a vault in the archives of the House of Lords, as it has for more than a century, sharing shelf space with three other British acts given royal assent and passage on March 29, 1867: *An Act to repeal the Duties of Assessed Taxes on Dogs*; *An Act for removing Doubts as to the Validity of certain marriages between British Subjects at Odessa*; and *An Act for the establishment in the Metropolis for Asylums for the Sick, Insane, and other Classes of the Poor*.

That vault, together with another deep inside the Victoria Tower of the British House of Parliament, is jammed with approximately 63,000 original acts of Britain's Parliament, many handwritten on parchment, rolled up, and placed on open shelves. Each is filed in the chronological order it was passed, going back to 1497 and the reign of King Henry VII.

The forty-seven-page BNA Act is printed on fine calfskin vellum and bound with a wrinkled red ribbon, and is stored inside a thin red hard cardboard box. It measures thirty-four by twenty centimetres, slightly larger than a magazine. *Ottawa Citizen* reporter Ian MacLeod, who visited London in 1999 to examine the document, wrote that "the title page is beginning to take on the weathered look of a pirate map."

The document, which he referred to as the "birth certificate" that brought the federation into existence, has a title page that boldly proclaims "An Act for The Union of Canada, Nova Scotia, and New Brunswick and the Government thereof; and for Purposes connected therewith."

On the first inside page, in the upper-right-hand corner above the preamble, are four handwritten words in old Norman French. "Le Reyne le Veult" meaning "The Queen wishes it. Royal assent."

The original BNA Act is rarely signed out for viewing, although the Parliamentary Archives is happy to do so when asked and does regularly deal with requests for copying, says Mari Takayanagi, an archivist for the Parliamentary Archives at the House of Lords Record Office in London.

"We do actually get out the original BNA Act and copy it for people occasionally, as is proved by the fact that we now keep a photocopy of it with the Act itself so we can make further copies from that, and avoid wear and tear on the original Act itself," says Takayanagi.

Over the years, some Canadians have said the original copy of record of the Act should be brought permanently to Canada and put on public display in Ottawa, like the Americans' revered exhibition in Washington, D.C., of the original Declaration of Independence, the U.S. Constitution, and the Bill of Rights.

"I've always thought it so colonial the fact that our most important document is outside the country," former Ottawa mayor Jim Watson told the *Ottawa Citizen* in 1999. At one point, Watson wrote Britain's then-prime minister, Margaret Thatcher, asking Britain to consider giving the Act to Canada. There was no reply.

"It's a bee in my bonnet," says Watson. "I just found it a little bizarre that the document, which symbolizes really the birth of our country, is not located in our country, that this document is hidden away in some room in London, not available for the Canadian public to see."

• • • First Flag Over Parliament Hill: Canadian Turning Point

The original Maple Leaf flag that first flew over Parliament Hill in 1965 is available for all to see at the Canadian Museum of Civilization in Gatineau, Quebec, until the end of 2006, when it is scheduled to be returned to its permanent display on Parliament Hill.

But Canadians with a flag fetish might be surprised by what they see. The red colouring of the original version is not as deep as the flag they've been familiar with for many years, and the seams are not entirely straight.

"It's just not as squared as we might expect," says David Monaghan, curator of the House of Commons. "While showing some minor signs of wear, including dirt, the flag is in excellent condition."

The colour difference reflects a change in the colour specification over the years, not the fading of the flag itself, adds Monaghan.

The imperfections may also be the result of quick mass production more than four decades ago, when, in the weeks leading up to the Parliament Hill ceremony that ushered in the new flag on February 15, 1965, the government of Lester Pearson placed a rush order for about twelve thousand Maple Leaf flags.

Visitors who viewed the flag when it was on display in the Centre Block at Parliament Hill in 2005 immediately noticed that the flag was a slightly different colour, said Monaghan.

Canadians have access to the first red and white maple leaf banner thanks to the dogged determination of *Ottawa Citizen* reporter Ian MacLeod, who tracked it down in Europe after a lengthy investigation.

Soon after it was taken down from its inaugural run up the pole ninety-two metres above Parliament Hill in 1965, it disappeared from public sight until MacLeod found it in a Belgian closet in 2005.

It had been tucked away in the Brussels home of Elizabeth Hoffmann-Lamoureux, the second wife of the late Lucien Lamoureux, the mid-1960s deputy House of Commons Speaker who had received it as a gift for his adept handling of the fiery debate over the design of a new flag.

After balking initially, she turned the flag over to Canada's ambassador in Belgium in time for Prime Minister Paul Martin to hold it aloft,

Lost for many years, Canada's first flag was rediscovered in 2005 and is now well cared for in Ottawa and available for all to see.

still folded for fear of damage, in front of thousands of spectators on Parliament Hill on Canada Day 2005.

On February 15, 2006, Ms. Hoffmann-Lamoureux joined new Prime Minister Stephen Harper, MPs, and senators at an invitation-only ceremony at which the 2.5-by-4.5-metre flag was unveiled in a giant 4-by-6-metre display case in the Hall of Honour in the Centre Block at Parliament Hill. Just prior to Canada Day 2006, it was moved across the Ottawa River to the Canadian Museum of Civilization in Gatineau, where it was displayed alongside the last Red Ensign.

"The flag is symbolic of a major event of Canadian history ... a turning point in our development as a nation," says Monaghan. "As a nation it also brought to close a difficult period of debate. Remember, the new flag was not universally accepted."

It may be taken on a cross-Canada tour with the other flags, said David Morrison, the museum's director of archaeology and history.

For more information visit www.civilization.ca.

WORTH NOTING...

On the day Canadians first saw the red Maple Leaf flag flown from a flagpole, two flags were raised, one atop the Peace Tower, another on a pole near the base of the tower. The smaller flag raised at ground level has never been found.

AND ANOTHER THING...

In 1965, the two Red Ensigns replaced by the new Maple Leaf flags were given to the National Museum of Canada, now the Canadian Museum of Civilization. One of them is on display until the end of 2006.

• • • "In Flanders Fields": Finding the Original Manuscript

"In Flanders Fields," written by Lieutenant-Colonel John McCrae, a Guelph, Ontario–born medical doctor, soldier, and poet, is one of the First World War's best-known poems.

Penned by McCrae on May 3, 1915, during the Second Battle of Ypres, the poem was published anonymously seven months later in England's *Punch Magazine*.

In her book *A Crown of Life: The World of John McCrae*, author Dianne Graves of Almonte, Ontario, writes, "In just 15 lines, John McCrae had captured the prevailing mood at the front."

The whereabouts of the original copy of "In Flanders Fields" that was delivered to *Punch Magazine* are unknown. However, later versions written by McCrae do exist.

Library and Archives Canada in Ottawa has two copies in its possession. One, signed by McCrae and dated December 8, 1915, is written in pencil on yellow paper and is part of a collection of documents donated to the archives by Edward Whipple Bancroft Morrison, a fellow officer and friend of McCrae's.

Courtesy of Guelph Civic Museum, McCrae House

John McCrae's famous poem is missing in action.

The second is typed on paper and is part of the collection of documents donated to the archives by James Edward Hervey MacDonald, an original member of Canada's Group of Seven painters.

Another copy is part of the collection at the Osler Library of the History of Medicine at McGill University in Montreal, where McCrae was once a pathology fellow. It is in McCrae's hand and is inscribed to May Metcalfe, a nurse at the Royal Victoria Hospital in Montreal.

The Osler Library also has a copy written by Dr. Edward Archibald, a surgeon who served in the war with McCrae. This version was sent to Dr. Archibald's wife, Agnes.

WORTH NOTING...

McCrae is long gone and so, it appears, is the original version of his poem, but the home where he was born in 1872 is still around for all to see. McCrae House, a small limestone cottage in Guelph, Ontario, has been preserved as a museum with exhibits, including McCrae's war medals, items from his medical practice, and other poems he wrote that interpret the life and times of McCrae. For more information call (519) 836-1221 or visit guelpharts.ca/mccraehouse.

Canada's famous poet grew up in this Guelph home, which is now a museum.

• • • The Flying Mile:
Canada's First Mechanical Ski Tow

When Canada's first mechanical ski lift pulled a load of skiers to the top of Mont Tremblant in Quebec's Laurentian Mountains on February 12, 1939, members of the news media struggled to find a name for the revolutionary contraption.

Some called it a teleferic, others referred to it as a cable chair, and still others named it a cable chair lift, a ski chair, and a ski lift. Finally, reporters came up with a name that combined a little of each: Aerial Ski Chair Ropeway.

Canada's first motorized ski tow, installed at Mont Tremblant, Quebec, by American millionaire Joe Ryan, was the second of its kind in North America; the first was built at Sun Valley in Idaho.

The Mont Tremblant lift was named after a racehorse owned by Ryan. Flying Mile was also the name of the first run cleared by Ryan at the popular ski resort, which is 130 kilometres northwest of Montreal.

The single chair lift, built by the U.S. Steel Company in Philadelphia, could transport 250 skiers per hour to the Mountain Lodge, about 272 metres from the base of the mountain.

Courtesy of Ron Booth

One surviving Flying Mile ski chair was made into a backyard swing in British Columbia.

From here, downhillers had access to four runs, Flying Mile, Simon Cooper, Sir Edward Beatty, and Nansen, according to *Mont Tremblant: Following the Dream*, published in 1998 by Louise Arbique, in collaboration with Marc Blais.

In the 1970s the lift's seats were replaced with a more modern and comfortable material, but the need to move more skiers to the top faster led to its demise. In 1981, when a triple chair was installed, Flying Mile was dismantled and sold to Ski Morin Heights, which is located in the St. Sauveur Valley, sixty kilometres north of Montreal.

Ski Morin Heights planned to use Flying Mile lift to bring skiers from a lower parking lot to the base of the mountain, but the project never got off the ground, and for many years the historic Mont Tremblant lift lay in a heap. For a time, several of the chairs were used for seating in a boutique at the resort.

Eventually, most remaining parts of the lift, including its large metal towers, were cut up for scrap.

However, at least one of Flying Mile's chairs has survived. It's owned by Ron Booth, who grew up in the Mont Tremblant area and as a young skier often rode Flying Mile up the mountain in the mid-1950s.

Now a resident of West Vancouver, Booth acquired the chair from Ski Morin Heights in the 1970s and converted it into a swing that for many years was used by his daughters in the backyard of the family's West Coast home.

In 2003, the swing was removed and stored behind a garage at Booth's summer property on Bowen Island, a community twenty minutes by ferry from West Vancouver.

In the summer of 2006, Booth planned to restore the chair as an outdoor swing for his grandson.

WORTH NOTING...

Flying Mile was lightning fast in its day, moving 250 skiers an hour to the mountain's mid-station, where another lift was installed later to take them to the summit at a height of 875 metres. But by today's standards it was a snail: Télécabine Express, a gondola installed at Mont Tremblant in 1998, carries 2,800 skiers per hour.

Courtesy of Station Mont Tremblant

The Flying Mile was ahead of its time.

• • • The Franks Flying Suit:
Condoms and Mice Helped Develop
the First Anti-Gravity Suit Used in War

Early in the Second World War, researchers led by Canadian medical pioneer Sir Frederick Banting discovered that fighter pilots frequently crashed as they pulled out of steep turns high in the sky.

As their aircraft accelerated, centrifugal force pushed blood into their legs and abdomens and it became too heavy to be pumped by the heart to the eyes and brains, causing pilots to black out or lose consciousness and, in either case, to lose control of their airplanes.

Banting immediately recognized that if pilots could avoid these conditions during dogfights miles up in the sky, Allied crews would have a tremendous tactical advantage.

Enter Dr. Wilbur Rounding Franks, a medical doctor and cancer researcher at the Banting and Best Medical Research Institute at the University of Toronto.

Using condoms fashioned into tiny water-filled G-suits for mice, Dr. Franks and his fellow researchers demonstrated that the rodents could tolerate up to 240 Gs without being harmed.

It was a huge breakthrough, and soon after, Dr. Franks and his team developed overalls made of two layers of rubber with water in between, which laced tight to the pilot's body. The getup was the Franks Flying Suit Mark I, the world's first G-suit used in combat.

The researchers later developed improved versions, including the Franks Flying Suit Mark III, an air-inflated, zippered design that squeezed the stomach and legs. The Mark III led directly to the first production model.

Although cumbersome and impractical, the initial design

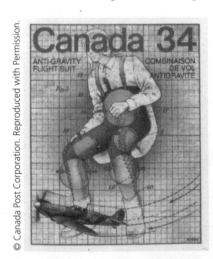

A 1986 Canada Post stamp commemorated Dr. Wilbur Franks's development of the flying suit.

protected pilots from forces of six Gs or more when the downward pressure on the water caused by acceleration created enough force to counteract the downward rush of blood in the body, helping pilots maintain consciousness.

In May 1940, Franks donned this first rough version of his Franks Flying Suit and climbed into a Fleet Finch trainer aircraft at Camp Borden near Barrie, Ontario, north of Toronto. When he and the pilot were hit with about seven Gs while pulling out of a steep dive, the pilot experienced a temporary blackout but Franks did not.

After the suit was modified to cover only the essential areas of the lower body, it was worn by a Royal Air Force pilot, D'Arcy Greig, who flew a Spitfire at Malton Airport in Toronto to become the first pilot to wear a true G-suit in flight. In the spring of 1941, Royal Canadian Air Force Squadron Leader F.E.R. Briggs became the first Canadian pilot to test the suit.

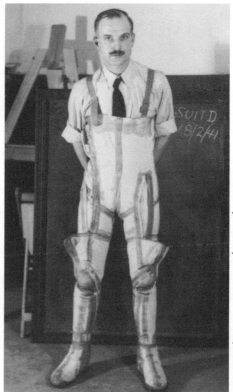

The Franks Flying Suit had its first battle test in 1942, when carrier-based fighter planes from the British Fleet Air Arm swept into Oran in French North Africa. By all accounts it was a success: "Because test pilots no longer blacked out during dangerous maneuvers, they could make observations which led to safer, stronger aircraft," said one report.

Peter Allen, a former commercial airline pilot who wrote a paper on the early years of Canadian aviation medicine for the Canadian Aviation Historical Society's *Journal*, compared Canada's development of early G-suits to the

Franks demonstrates his flying suit.

Courtesy of Library and Archives Canada, PA-063923

U.S. Apollo space program. Modern G-suits, including those worn by astronauts, use the same physiological principle applied by Dr. Franks.

A 1969 article in *Aerospace Medicine* described the Franks suit as a "rather remarkable Word War II achievement of aeromedical research and development." Reporting on a comparison of the combat effectiveness between fighter pilots who used the suit and those who did not, the publication said G-suit–equipped pilots shot down 81 percent more enemy planes per 1,000 sorties and 103 percent more per 10,000 operational hours than those not equipped with the suits.

Between 1940 and 1944 more than 250 modifications were made, and when the suit was manufactured for the British Ministry of Aircraft Production in the early 1940s, it was available in seven standard sizes.

The first G-suit, which stretched from high on the neck to toes and fingertips, was secretly sewn together by a tailor on an old sewing machine in Franks's office. A version of that suit is part of the collection at the Base Borden Military Museum in Barrie, Ontario. Although it has been on display in recent years, both at the Base Borden museum and off-site, it is not available for public viewing because of its fragility, says retired Lieutenant Colonel Stuart L. Beaton, the museum's director.

"It is made from cotton and rubber, which sixty-five years ago was not the greatest," says Beaton. "If you picked it up it might fall apart."

Beaton is hopeful that the museum will eventually acquire funds to build a case that would protect the historic suit from the ravages of temperature, humidity, and human hands and allow the public to view it.

Other versions of the Franks Flying Suit have also been preserved. One can be viewed by the public at the Canadian Warplane Heritage Museum in Hamilton, Ontario (www.warplane.com); another is part of the collection of Defence Research and Development Canada in Toronto (www.toronto.drdc-rddc.gc.ca) but is not on public display; and two more are in storage at the Canadian War Museum in Ottawa (www.warmuseum.ca) and are unavailable for viewing.

An exact replica is on display at the Toronto Aerospace Museum (www.torontoaerospacemuseum.com).

WORTH NOTING...

Ironically, an air crash took the life of Sir Frederick Banting. In 1941, while on his way to Britain to discuss aviation medicine and demonstrate the Franks Flying Suit Mark II, Banting died when his plane went down in Labrador. In 1921–22, Banting was part of the team that discovered insulin, a life-saving therapy for diabetes.

IN CASE YOU WERE WONDERING...

Dr. Franks, who died on January 4, 1986, also co-invented the RCAF Human Centrifuge, described by some as a high-speed merry-go-round, which was used to simulate G-forces at high speeds to train pilots in manoeuvring combat aircraft under G-force pressure. It was the forerunner of a larger one built by the U.S. Navy (with the assistance of Franks and Professor D. N. Cass-Beggs of the Department of Electrical Engineering) and used in the training of astronauts. For his efforts in aviation medicine, Franks received considerable recognition, including Officer of the Order of the British Empire in 1944.

AND ANOTHER THING...

G-suits for non-aviation purposes have been around since the early 1900s, when American Dr. George Crile invented a pneumatic suit that could be used to help stabilize patients who had gone into shock. Dr. Crile later collaborated with the U.S. Navy and the Goodyear Tire and Rubber Company to modify the pneumatic suit for use by military pilots.

• • • Canada's First Grain Elevator: Some Remnants Remain

The first grain elevator built on Canada's prairies was erected in 1879 next to the railway tracks in Niverville, Manitoba, a town of 2,300 people thirty kilometres south of Winnipeg.

Unfortunately, like many of its counterparts, this elevator has been all but erased from the prairie landscape. We dug deep, however, and found remnants of the historic building.

Unlike the rectangular structures that grace postcards and souvenir T-shirts, the 25,000-bushel Niverville elevator was silo-like in shape and topped with a peaked turret.

The historic wooden elevator was torn down in 1923, and some of the wood was used to build a barn on a farm in the community of Otterbourne, Manitoba, fourteen kilometres south of Niverville. In 2003, the barn was torn down. Luckily, a resident of the farm knew the origins of the wood and saved it from being burned or sent to a landfill site.

Courtesy of Niverville Heritage Centre

Today, a grain elevator and storage shed sit on the site where the Niverville elevator once looked over the community. The remaining pieces of the structure — mostly eighteen-inch-wide planks, silvery in colour with hints of red paint from their former life as a prairie barn — are being stored under a protective cover at a business in Niverville, says Steven Neufeld, chief

Canada's first wooden grain elevator was torn down in 1923, but bits of it still exist in Saskatchewan.

operating officer of the Niverville Heritage Centre, who helped save the wood when he was a member of town council.

"It's about enough wood to fill a pickup truck," he says.

The townspeople are attempting to raise $6.5 million to fund a new heritage centre complex, which will house a seniors' centre, a community centre, and other facilities.

Once the new centre is built, the remaining pieces of the Niverville elevator will be used as part of a commemorative wall in the complex's atrium to recognize donors to the project. Construction is slated to begin in October 2006.

Previously, some of the wood was used to make souvenir plaques, one of which was given to former Niverville resident Ben Sawatzky, who made a sizeable donation to the heritage centre project.

• •

Canada's Oldest Grain Elevator

The oldest standing grain elevator in Canada is located in Fleming, Saskatchewan, a tiny community on the Trans-Canada Highway about three kilometres west of the Manitoba border.

The Fleming elevator was built in 1895 by Lake of the Woods Milling

Courtesy of Bernard Flaman, Government of Saskatchewan

The oldest standing grain elevator in Canada is located in eastern Saskatchewan near the Manitoba border.

Company, according to the records of the Saskatchewan Wheat Pool, which later owned the building.

The elevator — consisting of wood crib construction, with a structural timber-on-concrete foundation, metal-clad exterior, and wood shingle roof — was used to store wheat until the late 1970s, when it was converted to a bulk fertilizer plant by United Grain Growers, says Bernard Flaman, heritage architect with Saskatchewan's Department of Culture, Youth and Recreation.

The elevator went out of service prior to 2000 because as a grain elevator it was too small, and as a fertilizer plant, the shift to more liquid fertilizers made it nonviable. Also, with the movement of grain over the years, the elevating equipment, the bins, and ultimately the whole elevator had worn out.

The Fleming elevator is being restored and is expected to be declared a Provincial Heritage Property. Possible uses include a tourist attraction or a tourist information office. It is owned by the Town of Fleming.

• •

AND ANOTHER THING...

In 1933 there were nearly 5,500 licensed primary grain elevators in Western Canada, more than half of them in Saskatchewan. In 2006, less than four hundred were still standing, thanks to the grain industry's move toward increased efficiency. Some of the elevators were replaced with computerized concrete monstrosities with eight times the holding capacity.

• • • The Largest Meteorite Found in Canada: Rock On

A meteorite discovered near the town of Madoc, Ontario, about two hundred kilometres west of Ottawa, is the largest ever found in Canada.

It surfaced on farmland northwest of the shore of Moira Lake in the autumn of 1854 and was recognized by William Logan, first director of the Geological Survey of Canada (GSC). The meteorite was reportedly being used to prop up a farm building.

It is a single mass of iron, originally weighing 167.8 kilograms, and classified as a type IIIAB (medium octahedrite). Although no one saw it streak through the sky, it is believed to have landed less than fifty years before it was found.

The Madoc meteorite was acquired by the GSC in 1855 as the first addition to the National Meteorite Collection. It was almost immediately exhibited at the 1855 Universal Exposition in Paris and is now on display in Logan Hall, National Resources Canada, at 601 Booth Street in Ottawa, where the public is welcome to drop by for a peek.

Other meteorites that have fallen in Canada weigh more in total but are from larger masses that disintegrated into many individual fragments, all smaller and lighter than the one found near Madoc.

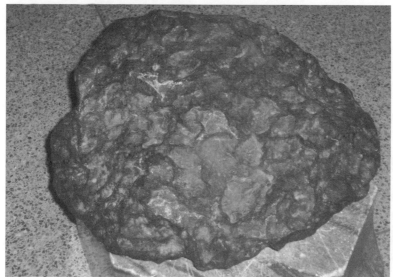

Famous meteorite on display in Ottawa.

Photo by Robert Vance

• • • Pistol Puzzler: The Weapons of Choice from Canada's Last Fatal Duel

On June 13, 1833, at about 6 p.m., two shots rang out on the banks of the Tay River on the edge of Perth, Ontario. When the smoke cleared, Robert Lyon, a nineteen-year-old law clerk, lay dead on the ground.

Thirty feet away stood John Wilson, twenty-three, who fired the fatal shot in what history records as Canada's last fatal duel.

The shootout was the result of a dispute over a lady, Elizabeth Hughes. Wilson claimed that Lyon was spreading word that Hughes was allowing young men "to indulge in little freedoms what were unbecoming."

Upset at this, Lyon later met Wilson, also a law clerk, in front of the court house and slapped his face. After consultation with friends, Wilson challenged Lyon to a duel, according to an undated report believed to have been written for the Perth Historical and Antiquarian Society about 1900.

On the day of the duel, a sunny and bright evening according to one account, sultry and rainy said another report, each man fired and missed.

Both were willing to give up, but Henry Le Lievre, a relative of Lyon's, would not allow the dispute to end without bloodshed. The pistols were reloaded and the principals again stood in place. At a word, both pistols exploded together, and Lyon crumpled to the ground, mortally wounded.

Courtesy of the Perth Museum

The duel pistols safe and sound in a Perth, Ontario, museum.

Wilson was jailed for three months on a charge of murder and later, after representing himself at trial in Brockville, Ontario, was set free. He eventually married Hughes and became a distinguished lawyer and a judge of the Supreme Court.

Lyon was buried in Perth's Craig Street Cemetery, also known as the Old Burying Ground, where his gravestone can be seen today.

The wood and metal percussion cap smooth bore duelling pistols, taken from a store in Perth and returned following the duel, were for some time owned by George Byron Lyon Fellowes, a nephew of Lyon's who witnessed the shooting.

Today they are in the collection of the Perth Museum, a gift from Kenyon Fellowes of Ottawa, a relative of the deceased Mr. Lyon, says the book *The Memorable Duel at Perth*, written by Edward Shortt.

In 1974, the pistols were stolen from the museum and later recovered by police in the backyard of a home in Perth. Since then, they have been safe and sound and can be viewed during regular museum hours.

For more information about the duel and pistols visit www.superaje.com/~perth.museum.

• • • *Ripley's It Happened in Canada*: Cartoon History

In the 1960s, '70s, and '80s, Gord Johnston's cartoons could be seen just about everywhere in Canada. Johnston, who was a political cartoonist in Ottawa from 1953 to the early 1960s, and for a time was an artist at the *Ottawa Citizen*, was the man behind the *It Happened in Canada* series of historical cartoons.

Samples of Gord Johnston's cartoons are part of Library and Archives Canada's collection.

His work, which at its peak appeared in seventy-one Canadian newspapers and was later reproduced in several books, consisted of cartoons and a few paragraphs of text packaged together to enliven Canadian history.

Subject matter included everything from a budgie in British Columbia with a 250-word vocabulary to a woman in Prince Edward Island who escaped hanging because nobody wanted to do the deed.

Johnston, a native of Tillsonburg, Ontario, lived in Ottawa with his daughter and his wife, Pat, until 1961, when he moved to London, Ontario. In the late 1970s, the name of the cartoon was changed to *Ripley's It Happened in Canada*, says Pat. He produced his cartoons until 1981 and died in London on August 3, 1983.

Although many of Johnston's original cartoons were destroyed, 637 samples of his work are part of the Library and Archives Canada collection in Ottawa, where the public can view them.

For more information visit www.collectionscanada.ca.

• • • St. Lawrence Hall Hotel:
An Assassin's Home Away from Home

It was the Montreal hotel where spies from the Confederate states hatched plots during the American Civil War and where John Wilkes Booth might have discussed his plan to assassinate Abraham Lincoln.

The St. Lawrence Hall Hotel, opened in 1851 at the northwest corner of St. James and St. Francois Xavier streets, was considered the finest hotel in Canada. An advertisement from the time described it as "furnished in the best style of New York and Boston hotels" and located in "the quiet, salubrious and fashionable part of the city."

Military leaders, prime ministers, and even the staff of the Prince of Wales, later King Edward VII, stayed in its rooms during its sixty-year history. It was said to be the only hotel in what was then Canada in the 1860s to have a bar that served mint juleps, perhaps reflecting its popularity with guests from the southern U.S.

But its most infamous visitor in the mid-1860s was Booth, an actor best known for shooting Lincoln in Ford's Theatre in Washington, D.C., in April 1865. Booth visited the hotel in the fall of 1864, ostensibly to set up some acting engagements and to check into oil investing, but quite possibly to discuss with the Confederate spies there how to kill the U.S. president.

According to the book *Montreal Yesterdays* by Edgar Andrew Collard, Booth was well liked by the hotel's owner, Henry Hogan, but others were not so impressed. In an account in the *Daily Witness*, someone who saw Booth at the St. Lawrence said that "his expenditure was profuse and reckless, and his habits intemperate." Booth apparently visited the hotel a couple of times, and according to Hogan, the would-be assassin stayed there just ten days before killing Lincoln.

Booth's fate is known by most, as he was hunted down and killed shortly after Lincoln's assassination. But what became of the Montreal hotel that he seemed to so enjoy?

Hogan ran the hotel until 1872, at which point it suffered from mismanagement and lost its place as the elite establishment of the city. Hogan returned, however, in 1879 to run the hotel again, refurbishing it to its previous glory. However, in the meantime, the Hotel Windsor took over as the number one lodging spot in Montreal, and the St. Lawrence was never quite the same.

Hogan died in his beloved hotel in 1902, and in 1910, the St. Lawrence was torn down so that the Dominion Express Company could build on the site.

• • • Superman Artwork: Missing in "Action"

Canadians may be familiar with their country's connection to Superman, the most famous comic book hero of the twentieth century. Although the caped crime fighter had a reputation for fighting for truth, justice, and the American way, he was the co-creation of a Canadian.

Joseph Shuster was born in 1914 in Toronto, Ontario, and at age nine moved with his family to Cleveland, Ohio. There, Shuster met future collaborator Jerry Siegel, and Shuster began making a name for himself as an artist writing an array of cartoons. In the mid-1930s the two began to provide DC Comics with such features as *Dr. Occult*, *Slam Bradley*, and *Radio Squad* before selling their most famous creation: Superman. The powerful superhero first appeared in DC's *Action Comics* #1 in 1938.

Shuster drew Superman through 1947, but eventually bad eyesight cut short his career. He died in 1992 of heart failure, but both he and Siegel had established their place in popular culture.

Copies of the *Action Comics* #1 are rare and reportedly worth up to almost $500,000 in mint condition. But what about Shuster's original artwork for Superman? Is it still around? We contacted several comic book experts and all doubted the drawing still existed.

A spokesperson at DC Comics says the policy there was always to return the artwork to the artist, and no record exists in its archives of the company having these drawings.

"My guess is that it is long lost," adds R.C. Harvey, a comic book expert. "I think the first published story was a cut-and-paste job: Shuster cut up daily comic strips and re-configured them into page format. The resulting messy appearance wouldn't have seemed precious to anyone seeing it at the print shop. And of course they tossed out stuff like that all the time."

Comic books weren't thought of as having value back then, he says. And while that attitude may have changed soon afterward, "I doubt, even then, that the artwork was considered valuable."

An interview with Shuster and Siegel by historian Tom Andrae printed in *NEMO: The Classics Comic Library* in 1983 does provide some insight into the two men behind Superman. In the interview,

Shuster mentions that rough drafts were usually done in pencil, and he noted that the first issue of *Action Comics* came about "very fast":

> They made the decision to publish it and said to us, "Just go out and turn out 13 pages based on your strip." It was a rush job, and one of the things I like least to do is to rush my artwork. I'm too much of a perfectionist to do anything which is mediocre. The only solution Jerry and I could come up with was to cut up the strips into panels and paste the panels on a sheet the size of the page. If some panels were too long, we would shorten them — cut them off — if they were too short, we would extend them.

Shuster also mentions an earlier prototype drawing of Superman done in 1933, which was reprinted in *NEMO* along with the interview showing the comic book hero without a cape and wearing a strongman's outfit. The story that went along with it was presumably destroyed.

While the artwork for the *Action Comics* #1 may no longer exist, Superman certainly lives on for comic book lovers everywhere. The summer 2006 release of *Superman Returns* starring Brandon Routh has confirmed the superhero's longevity with fans. And in addition to the

Photo by Mark Kearney

Man of Steel artwork made for popular comic book covers. Unfortunately the original artwork from 1938 seems to have disappeared.

popular 1950s TV series based on the comic book and the 1970s movies that starred the late Christopher Reeve, the 1990s saw a comic book on the "death" of Superman and his subsequent return and marriage to long-time flame Lois Lane. Both Canada Post and the U.S. Postal Service have issued a Superman stamp — in 1995 in Canada and in 1998 south of the border. The U.S. Postal Service announced in 2006 the issuance of commemorative DC Comics superhero stamps, including two of Superman.

AND ANOTHER THING...

If you linked that Shuster name with another famous Canadian, you're correct! Joe Shuster was the cousin of Frank Shuster, the famous comedian who achieved international success with partner Johnny Wayne.

TRANSPORTATION
• • •
How We Got Around

• • • Casey Baldwin's Airplane: First in Flight

Frederick "Casey" Baldwin gained fame on March 12, 1908, when he flew about 97 metres (319 feet) in a biplane over icy Keuka Lake in Hammondsport, New York. By doing so, Baldwin became the first Canadian to fly an airplane.

Though he wasn't the first to fly on Canadian soil — that would happen the following year when John McCurdy piloted the *Silver Dart* in Nova Scotia — Baldwin earned his place as one of the key pioneers in aviation history. His flight, watched by several spectators, is considered the first *public* heavier-than-air airplane flight in U.S. history. The Wright brothers' flight in 1903 was very much a private affair.

According to accounts, Baldwin got to fly the plane, named the *Red Wing*, because on the frigid day he was the only one of the aviation team who wasn't wearing ice skates. Since he was slipping on the ice, the others decided he would be most useful sitting in the cockpit. The flight had been more than a year in the making since Alexander Graham Bell established the Aerial Experiment Association (AEA), whose purpose was to build a practical airplane for $20,000.

The *Red Wing*, designed by American Thomas Selfridge and so named because of the red silk that covered its frame, flew only some five to ten feet off the ground during Baldwin's sojourn but made a smooth landing. There was a small story about the flight on the front page of the next day's *New York Times*, but Baldwin's name wasn't mentioned. The

Red Wing's final flight, five days later on March 17, was not as successful. A stiff breeze caught the plane after about 120 feet in the air and sent it and Baldwin to the ground. Although Baldwin escaped injury, the plane's motor and wing were damaged beyond repair.

Over the next two months, the AEA team built a second plane, the *White Wing*, which had considerable success. Accounts from the time make no mention of what happened to the wreckage of the *Red Wing*, however. Was any of it salvaged and used elsewhere? Or was it simply left to the elements? At any rate, the *Red Wing* remains a key piece of the history of flight, and photographs of it exist to this day.

Baldwin would go on to make more flights and sit as a politician in the Nova Scotia legislature before dying in 1948. Selfridge, unfortunately, suffered a cruel fate. In September 1908, during a flight in which he was a passenger, the plane crashed, severely injuring him. He later died in surgery, thus becoming the first airplane fatality in the world.

Frederick "Casey" Baldwin and John McCurdy. Baldwin made history when he flew in the Red Wing, but the plane crashed beyond repair in 1908.

• • • Canada's First Automobile: Full Steam Ahead

In 1867, Canada's first self-propelled automobile was demonstrated at the Stanstead Fair in the community of Stanstead Plain, Quebec, southeast of Montreal.

The vehicle, invented by watchmaker Henry Seth Taylor, was powered by steam, had no brakes, and could reach a top speed of just fifteen miles per hour.

Despite Taylor's pioneering efforts, it was the subject of considerable ridicule from townsfolk who considered it a "toy of exaggerated size and power," according to an article published by the Antique Automobile Club of America in 1968.

Nevertheless, a local newspaper called the steam car "the neatest thing of the kind yet invented" and Taylor boasted that his vehicle would challenge "any trotting horse."

The basis of the car, which Taylor started building in 1865, was a high-wheeled carriage with some bracing to support a two-cylinder steam engine mounted under the floor. Steam was generated in a vertical coal-fired boiler mounted at the rear of the vehicle behind the seat. The boiler was connected by rubber hoses to a six-gallon water tank located between the front wheels. Forward and reverse movements were controlled by a lever, and a vertical crank connected to the wheels was used for steering.

The vehicle's lack of brakes proved to be its undoing. After driving it for several years and showing it off at carnivals and parades, Taylor lost control one summer day as he drove down a hill. Before he came to a stop, the car had turned on its side, its wheels shattered.

Discouraged, Taylor put the remains in a barn near Stanstead Plain, where they sat until the early 1960s when Gertrude Sowden of Stanstead purchased the property. She recognized the value of Taylor's

A Canada Post stamp depicts Canada's first automobile, now stored in an Ottawa museum.

creation, but when she couldn't interest museums in it, she sold the remains to American Richard Stewart of Middlebury, Connecticut, president of Anaconda American Brass.

Eventually new wheels were made, the seat and dashboard were recovered with leather, all wooden parts were scraped, sanded, and repainted, and brakes were added. None of the engine parts needed replacing.

The Taylor steam car was acquired by the Canada Science and Technology Museum in Ottawa in 1984. Although it is on exhibit from time to time, the vehicle spends much of its time in a climate-controlled warehouse adjacent to the museum, where public access can be arranged by appointment.

In the summer of 2005, the vehicle was shown four times, twice to individuals and twice as part of a larger tour of the warehouse.

"Looking at the vehicle, one sees the origins of the automobile, even though it predates the blossoming of the auto industry by forty years," says Garth Wilson, curator of transportation at the Ottawa museum. "It is absolutely significant in that it is the first Canadian made auto and, as such, represents Canada's entry into the world of automobiles."

For more information, visit www.sciencetech.technomuses.ca or call (613) 991-3044.

WORTH NOTING...

There will always be debate over who invented the world's first self-propelled automobile, but one thing is certain: Canada's Henry Seth Taylor is in good company. The French say one of their countrymen, inventor Nicolas-Joseph Cugnot, built the world's first self-propelled mechanical vehicle, "Fardier à vapeur" (steam wagon), in 1769. German Karl Benz, generally thought to be the father of the practical motorcar in Europe, unveiled his first vehicle, a three-wheeled, gas-powered car known as "Benz Patent Motor Car" in 1886. American Henry Ford's initial vehicle was the gasoline-powered Quadracycle, first sold in 1896.

• • • Bombardier's Brainchild: The First Snowmobile

Joseph-Armand Bombardier had been in the business of producing vehicles that travelled on snow since 1937, but it wasn't until 1959 that the Valcourt, Quebec, inventor produced the machine that would revolution-ize winter sports in Canada and other northern countries.

After many years of testing, Bombardier and his team, including his son Germain, unveiled the little yellow sled that led to the birth of an industry. His invention was the lightweight and easy to operate snow-mobile, which was powered by a reliable two-cycle engine and utilized a seamless, wide caterpillar track that incorporated steel rods patented by his son. Known as the Ski-Doo, it was an instant hit.

The February 1963 issue of *Imperial Oil Review* described the machine as a "kind of scooter mounted on toy tracks and which growls like a runaway dishwasher." It opened up communities across Northern Canada in winter and introduced Canadians to a new winter sport — snowmobiling.

Unfortunately, Bombardier never had the opportunity to see the success the Ski-Doo and his company would later enjoy. He died of cancer on February 18, 1964, at the age of fifty-six, at a time when his company held more than forty patents and was registering sales of $10 million.

The first twenty-five snowmobiles built by Bombardier in 1959 were made by hand; the first one built was given to his friend Maurice

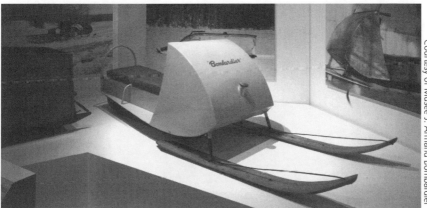

Courtesy of Musée J. Armand Bombardier

The first snowmobile ever built is in a Valcourt, Quebec, museum.

Ouimet, a Marie-Immaculée oblate and missionary among the Ojibwa peoples of Lansdowne House in northern Ontario.

That vehicle, marked with serial number K-1 and equipped with wooden skis, a one-speed forward transmission, and a four-stroke, seven-horsepower Kohler engine that enabled the machine to reach a maximum speed of forty kilometres per hour, was later acquired from Ouimet and is on display at the Musée J. Armand Bombardier in Valcourt, Quebec.

For more information, visit www.museebombardier.com or call (450) 532-5300.

WORTH NOTING...

A tragedy in the Bombardier family played a role in the invention of Joseph-Armand Bombardier's snow vehicles. In January 1934, Bombardier's two-year-old son Yvon needed immediate hospital treatment for appendicitis and peritonitis, but with roads blocked by snow in the Valcourt area, there was no way he could get the boy to the nearest hospital, fifty kilometres away in Sherbrooke, Quebec. The death of his son made Bombardier all the more determined to create a snow machine that would help avoid similar tragedies.

AND ANOTHER THING...

In the late 1950s, the list price of a Ski-Doo was about $900. Today's models range in price from $6,000 to $12,000.

Photo by Randy Ray

Today's snowmobiles are much sleeker and faster than their ancestors.

• • • The *Simcoe*: First Merchant Ship into the St. Lawrence Seaway System

The St. Lawrence Seaway opened for business on the morning of April 25, 1959, when the bulk carrier *Simcoe*, commanded by Captain Norm Donaldson, entered the waterway from the eastern end at the St. Lambert lock on the south shore of Montreal.

Simcoe, then owned by Canada Steamship Lines (CSL), was the first commercial vessel to transit the seaway, which had been five years in the making and soon became a vital artery that enabled industries in North America's heartland to compete in export markets.

Among *Simcoe*'s passengers was T.R. McLagan, president of CSL. Prime Minister John Diefenbaker was aboard Canadian Coast Guard icebreaker *d'Iberville*, which also entered the seaway on opening day.

Courtesy of the St. Lawrence Seaway Management Corporation

The *Simcoe* enters the St. Lambert lock in 1959. The ship was eventually scrapped.

At the time, the 259-foot-long *Simcoe* was a CSL stalwart entering her thirty-third year of service for the company. She and ships of her size would soon be replaced by much larger lakers designed to maximize the increased size allowances offered by the seaway.

The ship was built in England in 1923 by Swan, Hunter & Wigham Richardson Ltd. and was known as *Glencorrie* under its first two owners, Glen Line Ltd. of Midland, Ontario, and Geo. Hall Coal & Shipping Corp. of Montreal. In 1926, she was purchased by CSL and her name was changed to *Simcoe*.

During the Second World War, she was chartered by the Canadian government to transport supplies for the military and was one of a handful of bulk carriers to avoid being sunk by enemy torpedoes.

She was owned by CSL until 1961 before being sold to Simcoe Northern Offshore Drilling Ltd. of Kingston, where she was converted to a drilling barge and renamed *Nordrill*.

In 1977, eighteen years after making history as the first bulk carrier to enter the St. Lawrence Seaway, *Simcoe* was scrapped at Port Colborne, Ontario.

Courtesy of Library and Archives Canada, PA-47930

John Diefenbaker took part in the ceremony that sent *Simcoe* through the St. Lawrence Seaway.

WORTH NOTING...

Simcoe was the first merchant ship to enter the St. Lawrence Seaway but was not the first vessel to transit the waterway. That honour goes to the icebreaker *d'Iberville*, which entered the seaway on April 25, 1959, just ahead of *Simcoe*. Built in 1953 by Davie Shipbuilding & Engineering Co. Ltd. for Transport Canada's Canadian Marine Service (later known as the Canadian Coast Guard), *d'Iberville* spent much of her life in the Arctic, where she activated navigational aids and delivered supplies to outposts. She also escorted ships in the St. Lawrence River and cleared ice jams to prevent flooding. She was retired at the end of 1982, put up for sale a year later, and scrapped in Kaohsiung, Taiwan, in 1989.

• • • The Popemobile:
Designed to Withstand a Commando Attack

They were two Canadian-made vehicles specially adapted for Pope John Paul II's 1984 visit to Canada. Not surprisingly, they were known as "Popemobiles."

They were used during the late pope's September 1984 papal tour of Canada, after an assassination attempt in 1981 prompted the Vatican to demand more protection for the pontiff. One was also used by the Pope when he visited Cuba in 1998.

Both Popemobiles were built by Camions Pierre Thibault, a Pierreville, Quebec, emergency vehicle maker well known for its fire trucks. They're modified GMC Sierra Heavy-Duty V8 trucks with a large transparent dome designed to keep the Pope fully protected and comfortable, yet completely visible.

The dome area is fully air-conditioned and is upholstered in red velvet imported from France. The $15,000 trucks were donated by GM Canada, and the 3.2-centimetre-thick bulletproof glass is made of a special laminate valued at $42,000 and donated by GE Canada.

The cube area accommodated the Pope and four other people. The trucks were equipped with video cameras, which produced footage that

During his visit to Canada in 1984, the Pope travelled in the Popemobile, which protected him and allowed him see the crowds. This vehicle, pictured in Ottawa, is part of the collection of an Ottawa museum.

was sold to the media and used for security. The total cost for each vehicle was $130,000.

Originally the property of the Canadian Conference of Catholic Bishops, one Popemobile was donated to the Canada Science and Technology Museum in Ottawa in 1985, where it is occasionally on display. While in storage the vehicle can be viewed by appointment only by calling (613) 991-3044. The other Popemobile is at the Vatican in Rome.

• • • *Titanic*:
Canadian Morgue Ships Rescued Victims

Names like Charles Melville Hays and Harry Markland Molson are well-documented Canadian connections to the *Titanic* disaster. More than 1,500 lives were lost when the luxury liner struck an iceberg and sank off the coast of Newfoundland in April 1912.

Hays was president of the Grand Trunk Railway, later the Canadian National Railway; Molson was a fourth-generation member of the Montreal family that made a fortune brewing beer, banking, and building steamships.

Less well known are *Montmagny, Minia, Mackay-Bennett*, and *Algerine*.

They're the names emblazoned on four Canadian ships based in Atlantic Canada that had the melancholy task of recovering bodies after the *Titanic* sank to the bottom of the Atlantic Ocean.

Known as "morgue ships," *Montmagny, Minia*, and *Mackay-Bennett* were dispatched from Halifax, the closest major seaport with rail connections; the *Algerine* originated at St. John's.

Their role in the April 15 disaster left Halifax with a legacy of grim memories, recovered wreckage, funerals, and gravesites.

In total, the ships found 328 of the 335 bodies that did not go down with the ship. Recovery was hard, grim work, amidst large waves and

Courtesy of Library and Archives Canada, PA-77747

Algerine from Newfoundland found one body.

dangerous ice floes. Some crew were paid double and given extra rum rations, according to records obtained from Nova Scotia Archives and Records Management.

Like the *Titanic*, all four vessels are gone, mere memories of Northern Canada's maritime history.

The *Mackay-Bennett* was 270 feet long and 40 feet wide and was built in 1884 by John Elder and Co., in Glasgow, Scotland. She was launched in 1884 to maintain 6,500 nautical miles of communications cables laid beneath the Atlantic Ocean between Europe and North America.

On April 17, 1912, her role changed dramatically. With coffins, one hundred tons of ice, an undertaker, and a chaplain on board, *Mackay-Bennett* left Halifax and three days later arrived near the scene of the sinking. She found 306 bodies, so many that embalming fluid ran out and 116 corpses had to be buried at sea. With flags at half-mast and coffins stacked on the stern, *Mackay-Bennett* returned to Halifax to the tolling of church bells on April 30.

Mackay-Bennett continued at Halifax until 1922, when she was retired to Plymouth, England, and used as a cable storage hulk. During the Second World War, she was sunk at her moorings at the time of the blitz on Plymouth but was later refloated and refitted for cable storage, a task she carried out until September 1965, when she was towed away to be broken up at Ghent, Belgium.

Courtesy of the Collection of the Maritime Museum of the Atlantic

The *Mackay-Bennett* bringing back Titanic dead.

Minia was a 328.5-by-35.8-foot cable ship built in 1866 by London and Glasgow Company in Glasgow, Scotland. Among its operations over the years was the laying of telegraph cables in China and Panama. *Minia* departed Halifax on April 17 to relieve *Mackay-Bennett* and found seventeen bodies. In 1922, *Minia* was sold and later broken up.

Montmagny was built in a Canadian government shipyard in Sorel, Quebec, and launched in 1909 as a 213-by-35-foot steel lighthouse supply vessel and buoy tender. *Montmagny* found four bodies. Ironically, she suffered a similar fate as the *Titanic*. On September 18, 1914, while en route to supply lighthouses on the north shore of the Gulf of St. Lawrence, with lightkeepers and their families on board, she was rammed by the collier *Lingan*. The ship sank in four minutes, and fourteen people, including eleven children, lost their lives. The accident occurred within sight of the town for which she was named.

Algerine was built in Belfast, Ireland, in 1880 as a naval gunboat. In 1893, she was converted to a sealing ship by her new owner, the Bowring Group of Companies of St. John's, founders of the modern-day version of Bowring stores. After returning from the annual seal hunt in early May of 1912, *Algerine* was commissioned by White Star, owners of the *Titanic*, to help with the body search. *Algerine* left St. John's on May 15.

With Captain John Jackman in command, and a cargo of two embalmers, embalming fluid, and fifty coffins, for three weeks she circled the area where the *Titanic* sank, St. John's–based *Downhomer Magazine* reported in April 1998. The lone body found was that of James McGrady, a native of Ireland who was a steward on the *Titanic*. His corpse, found on May 27, was the final body recovered from the great ship.

In a cruel twist of fate, while hunting seals off Baffin Island, *Algerine* sank on July 15, 1912, three months to the day after the *Titanic* was lost.

WORTH NOTING...

There are 150 *Titanic* victims buried in Halifax. Of the 328 bodies recovered by Canadian vessels, 116 were buried at sea, usually because they were damaged or decomposed beyond preservation. It has been suggested that given the class attitudes of the times, most of these were third-class passengers and crew members. A total of 209 bodies were brought back to Halifax; 59 were claimed by relatives and shipped to their home communities. The remaining 150 victims are buried in three cemeteries: Fairview Lawn, Mount Olivet, and Baron de Hirsch, each open to the public.

• •

Titanic Artifacts Galore

Additional *Titanic* artifacts in Canada can be found at the Maritime Museum of the Atlantic, which has a large number of items in its Titanic Exhibit, most donated and some lent by descendants of Nova Scotians who were involved in recovering *Titanic* bodies. These include:

- a pair of small brown leather shoes, worn by an unknown child thought to be about two years old who died in the disaster. The shoes are displayed next to the gloves of railway tycoon Charles Hays, which were also recovered after *Titanic* sunk.

  "The shoes of a third-class infant will sit beside the gloves of a millionaire ... a reminder of the cross section of humanity which perished in this shipwreck," says Dan Conlin, curator of the Maritime Museum of the Atlantic.

  The little boy's body was brought home on the *Mackay-Bennett* and buried in Fairview Lawn Cemetery, where his gravestone has become one of Halifax's most famous memorials.

- a deck chair that bears a carved five-pointed star, the emblem of the White Star Line. Made of mahogany and unidentified hardwood, it is one of the only intact chairs in the world that matches those seen in *Titanic* photographs.

- lounge panelling that contains musical instruments and scroll in the Louis XV style used for the lounge. It comes from the arch over the forward entrance to the first-class lounge, the area where the *Titanic* broke in half just before plunging to the bottom.

- a newel post face from newel posts of either the forward or aft first-class staircase.

- oak trim with a vegetable, fruit, and flower design. Made of quarter-cut English white oak, its image is easily spotted

A sign points the way to one of three Halifax cemeteries that commemorate *Titanic* victims. All are open to the public.

in photographs, paintings, and movie recreations of the *Titanic*'s grand first-class staircase.

- ornamental oak from the sides of the balustrade of the forward first-class staircase. The "S"-shaped twist indicates it was from the portion of the staircase leading to the first-class reception room on D-Deck, where passengers gathered before meals in the nearby dining room.
- a cribbage board made by *Minia*'s ship's carpenter, William Parker, from a piece of oak taken from the water after *Titanic* sunk. It is typical of the crib boards, picture frames, and other practical knick-knacks made of *Titanic* wood by *Minia* crew members.

The Newfoundland Museum in St. John's is caretaker of the life jacket James McGrady was wearing, which has been a popular artifact since the release of James Cameron's epic movie *Titanic*.

For more information, visit the Newfoundland Museum (www.therooms.ca/museum) and the Maritime Museum of the Atlantic (www.museum.gov.ns.ca).

● ●

• • • First Train Across Canada: Chugging into History

On June 28, 1886, nearly eight months after the last spike was driven at Craigellachie, B.C., the first transcontinental Canadian Pacific Railways train left Montreal for the Pacific Ocean.

At noon hour on July 4, 1886, Train No. 1, the Pacific Express, with 150 passengers on board, rolled into Port Moody, B.C. It was an occasion one history book described as "the most significant event in the history of Port Moody." The 2,892.6-mile trip across four time zones took 139 hours.

Whatever happened to the train that made the first trip across Canada on the brand new east–west rail line?

For starters, only two of the ten cars that made up the train as it left Montreal — the *Honolulu*, a sleeper car, and Car 319, carrying mail, express, and baggage — made the entire westward journey. Other cars were picked up and dropped off along the way; as the train made its way across Canada, its locomotives were changed more than two dozen times.

Courtesy of City of Vancouver Archives

Historic Engine No. 374 has been restored and can be seen in Vancouver.

Locomotive 371, which was placed on the train at North Bend, B.C., just east of Port Moody, was the engine chosen to pull the first transcontinental train into the terminal at Port Moody, where Vancouver-bound passengers were transferred to a stage coach for the final twelve-mile leg of the trip.

According to the Canadian Pacific Archives, Locomotive No. 371, which was built in Montreal in 1886, was scrapped in October 1915. The baggage, mail/express car, which was built in 1884 by the CPR at its Hochelaga shops, was renumbered several times before being scrapped in 1937 at Montreal. The *Honolulu*, built in 1886 by Barney & Smith, was renamed *Pembroke* in 1918, renumbered 1705 in 1926, and then scrapped in 1930 at Montreal.

The first engine and rail cars to arrive at the west coast may be long gone, but another engine of significance is still intact and honoured for its historic role: Locomotive No. 374, which on May 23, 1887, became the first engine to haul a train into Vancouver once tracks were extended from Port Moody, is on display at the Roundhouse Community Arts and Recreation Centre in Vancouver.

The locomotive was extensively rebuilt in October 1915 and remained in service until July 1945, when it was retired and donated to the City of Vancouver, according to CP Archives.

In the 1980s, the West Coast Railway Association and the Canadian Railroad Historical Association undertook a round of cosmetic work that restored No. 374 to the way it looked in 1945.

For more information, visit www.roundhouse.ca or www.see-vancouverheritage.com/eng374/eng374.htm.

● ●

The Last Spike

Three spikes were connected to the historic ceremony that marked the completion of the CPR on November 7, 1885, at Craigellachie, B.C. We can tell you the whereabouts of two.

A silver spike, specially made for the ceremony for Lord Lansdowne, Canada's governor-general at the time, arrived in British Columbia several months before the rail line was finished and was never used. Two iron spikes, however, played a key role when east was welded to west at a point 2,554 miles east of Montreal and 338.5 miles west of Port Moody, B.C.

The first iron spike was bent when Donald Smith, a key financial supporter of the railway, attempted to drive it into a wooden railway tie; he successfully drove the second into the tie at 9:22 a.m. Pacific Time, but it didn't stay in place for long.

The bent spike was retrieved as a souvenir by Smith. He had a portion of it shaved off and ringed with diamonds as a gift for his wife, although other accounts say other women also received jewelry made from the spike.

It is part of the collection at the Canada Science and Technology Museum in Ottawa. It's four to five inches long, is cracked, and clearly shows where Smith had pieces shaved away. It is occasionally on display and has been lent to other museums.

The silver spike has been mounted on a marble base and is in Toronto, owned by descendants of the family of Cornelius Van Horne, general manager of the CPR at the time and later its president. Van Horne was in attendance when the last spike was driven.

The spike that went into the railway tie on Smith's second attempt was later removed and presented to Edward Beatty, who was appointed president of the CPR in 1918 and held the post for twenty-five years. Its location is unknown.

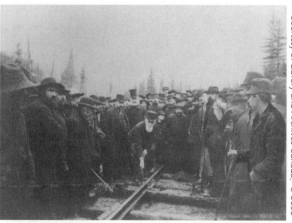

Courtesy of Library and Archives Canada, C-3693

Where is the spike that was hammered in at Craigellachie, British Columbia, on November 7, 1885?

• • • World's First Motorized Wheelchair

Recognizing the difficulties faced by veterans disabled in the Second World War, Canadian inventor George Johnn Klein invented the world's first electric wheelchair.

The Hamilton inventor, whom the *Canadian Encyclopedia* describes as "possibly the most productive inventor in Canada in the twentieth century," was able to overcome challenges faced by others with an innovative twenty-four-volt power system, separate and reversible drive units for each of the two main wheels, and an easy-to-use joystick-style control throttle.

The Canada Science and Technology Museum in Ottawa has called the wheelchair "one of the most significant artifacts in the history of Canadian science, engineering, and invention."

It was developed by Klein at the National Research Council of Canada (NRC) in Ottawa in collaboration with Veterans Affairs Canada and the Canadian Paraplegic Association. But, alas, the chair would be produced in the United States instead of Canada.

In the early 1950s, no Canadian manufacturers were able to mass-produce the device, so to promote the technology the electric prototype

Courtesy of National Research Council of Canada

George Klein, left, with the revolutionary motorized wheelchair he invented.

was presented to the United States Veterans Administration at the U.S. Embassy in Ottawa on October 26, 1955. A year later, a California company began churning out motorized wheelchairs.

The prototype wheelchair has been a coveted possession of the Smithsonian's National Museum of American History since 1979. However, it has been on display at the Canada Science and Technology Museum in Ottawa since 2005.

Over the years, countless people in Canada and around the world have benefited by having access to the Klein wheelchair.

"It has all of the elements of a significant invention," says Randall Brooks, assistant director of the Collection and Research Division at the Canada Science and Technology Museum. "It freed the disabled up to be independent because previously, anyone who did not have the use of one or both hands was completely reliant on someone else to get around. It allowed people to get out and work, to make a living and contribute to society."

Described in a June 2004 report in the *Ottawa Citizen* as "a clunky looking thing, a far cry from the sleek and speedy mobile machines used today," Klein's chair attracted international attention with its innovative controls, ease of operation, flexible drive system, and dependability.

Klein has been hailed as one of Canada's most remarkable engineers. He also invented medical suturing devices, Canada's first wind tunnel, and gearing systems for the Canadarm used on several U.S. space shuttle missions. He died in 1992.

For more information, visit the Smithsonian Institution at www.si.edu or the Canada Science and Technology Museum at www.sciencetech.technomuses.ca or call (613) 991-3044.

THE POLITICAL RING
• • •
Taking a Recount

• • • The Canada–United States Free Trade Agreement: Leaving Canadians Dazed and Confused

In the mid-1980s, the federal government's plan to negotiate a free trade agreement with the United States had Canada in an uproar.

Organized labour feared major job losses as businesses relocated to the U.S. or were crushed by increased competition from larger American firms. Canadian nationalists worried that further economic integration with the U.S would threaten Canadian culture and sovereignty.

Many Canadian businesses, on the other hand, favoured the trade pact, feeling it would provide improved and secure access to the U.S. market, which is ten times bigger than Canada's.

And ordinary Canadians? For the most part, they were dazed and confused by the raucous debate that raged across their nation.

The controversy — which at times threatened to split the country in two — is a distant memory, but the FTA, as it was known for short, and its effects on Canada's economy, linger.

Since the trade agreement was put into force on January 1, 1989, after being signed in 1988 by Prime Minister Brian Mulroney and U.S. President Ronald Reagan, proponents have boasted that it has done what was intended — promoted productivity and full employment and encouraged foreign direct investment in Canada.

They also say the FTA, and a follow-up agreement, the North American Free Trade Agreement (NAFTA), which brought Mexico into the free trade fold, has strengthened the competitiveness of Canadian firms in global markets and ensured the steady improvement of living standards.

The FTA included a schedule for the elimination of all tariffs on trade between Canada and the United States by January 1, 1998. It established a mutually beneficial framework for the fair and predictable treatment of investors. It also included rules governing trade in services.

In his 1998 paper "The Road to Free Trade," trade expert Michael Hart of the Centre for Trade Policy and Law at Carleton University in Ottawa opined that the two trade agreements, and pacts negotiated later, have been positive for Canada.

"With the exception of a few sectors such as dairy and poultry products, Canadian industry was considered ready to take on the world, at home and abroad ... Canadians in general seem content with the new direction. They have weathered the storm of adjustment and are beginning to reap the benefits of a more open economy."

Canadians who want to peruse the historic FTA document can do so on the Internet, but having a peek at the original document is out of the question. Canada's copies are in storage in a room known as the "treaty vault" on Floor C-7 in the Lester B. Pearson Building, at 125 Sussex Drive in Ottawa, a short drive from Parliament Hill.

That's the same room where hundreds of other treaties are kept, including Canada's version of the Treaty of Versailles, signed in 1919 to end the First World War; the March 1942 agreement between Canada and the U.S. to build the Alaska Highway; and a June 1952 pact dealing with construction of the St. Lawrence Seaway.

Also tucked away in the seventh-floor vault is Canada's copy of the North American Free Trade Agreement, signed in December 1992 between Canada, the United States, and Mexico. NAFTA formed the world's largest free trade area, effectively replacing the FTA.

Like all signed treaties, the FTA and NAFTA are legal-sized 8.5-by-14-inch documents bound with simple string binding. The FTA has a royal blue simulated leather cover embossed in gold with Canada's coat of arms. The FTA is about three inches thick and covers 236 pages; one copy is in French and the other is in English.

NAFTA was signed by Mulroney, U.S. President George Bush Sr., and Mexican President Carlos Salinas de Gortari on December 17, 1992. The treaty vault contains copies in English, French, and Spanish, each about three inches thick, but because it consists of considerably more chapters, annexes, and tariff schedules than the FTA, and has been amended on numerous occasions, it takes up about four feet of shelf space.

The trade pacts and many other historic treaties can be read at www.treaty-accord.gc.ca.

• • • Sir John A. Macdonald: His Legacy Lives On

Sir John A. Macdonald may be long gone, but Canada's first prime minister is certainly not forgotten in Kingston, Ontario, where he launched his political career.

Macdonald held the country's top elected post from 1867 to 1873 and from 1878 to 1891. Those with an interest in the flamboyant political leader will find plenty of landmarks in Kingston that commemorate the life and times of Macdonald, who, in addition to being on the city's municipal council and a member of the Legislative Assembly of Canada in 1844, was a successful lawyer and businessman, holding directorships with at least ten companies.

In a career smattered with controversy, Macdonald's achievements include the confederation of the colonies of the United Province of Canada (Ontario and Quebec), Nova Scotia, and New Brunswick into the Dominion of Canada in 1867.

Courtesy of Library and Archives Canada, C-2090

Sir John A. spent many years in Kingston, Ontario.

His policy of westward expansion resulted in a transcontinental nation in 1871 and the construction of the Canadian Pacific Railway by 1885. When the Glasgow, Scotland–born Macdonald died, the foundation for the nation had been well laid, despite his penchant for heavy drinking and his involvement in controversies, including his acceptance of large campaign contributions from Sir Hugh Allan, which were later considered bribes when Macdonald awarded Allan's syndicate the contract to build the CPR.

Kingston boasts all kinds of landmarks to its famous son:

- 110-112 Rideau Street is the house where Macdonald lived as a teenager and at age fifteen began training for the legal profession as an apprentice. It's now a private residence marked with a plague that reads "SIR JOHN ALEXANDER MACDONALD, 1851–1891 Statesman and Patriot. His boyhood days, those critical years that decide the character of the man, were spent in the Old Town, which has seen more than a Century of Canadian History. Erected by the National Committee for the Celebration of the Diamond Jubilee of Confederation, A. D. 1927."
- 169-171 Wellington Street became in 1835 Macdonald's first law office, where he later took in two law students, Oliver Mowat and Alexander Campbell, both of whom later became Fathers of Confederation. The building, now a diner, has a plaque affixed to the outside that notes its significance.
- Bellevue House, at 35 Centre Street, was Macdonald's home from August 1848 to September 1849. Staffed by costumed interpreters, the house and gardens were restored and are kept much as they would have been during the time that Macdonald lived there with his wife, Isabella, and infant son. A month after the couple moved into Bellevue House, their thirteen-month-old baby died.
- 180 Johnson Street: built in 1843, it housed Macdonald and his wife from 1849 to 1852. Their second son, Hugh John, was born in the house in 1850. The building is now a private home and is marked with a plaque.
- 343 King Street East: Macdonald's law office between 1849 and 1860. Although he was away from Kingston for extensive periods in his role as

Sir. John A. Macdonald lived in Bellevue House in Kingston for about a year. It is now a popular tourist attraction.

Courtesy of Kingston Economic Development Corporation

MP, Macdonald retained his partnership in the Kingston law firm until 1871. The building is marked with a plaque and in 2006 housed a gourmet pizza restaurant.

- 79-81 Wellington Street is marked with a plaque indicating that Macdonald rented this double house from 1876 to 1878 for his sister Louisa and his brother-in-law James Williamson, a professor at Queen's. According to author Margaret Angus's book *John A. Lived Here*, the 1877 assessment roll lists Macdonald as a resident in this house, which was in his name.

- Macdonald is buried at the Cataraqui Cemetery on Purdy Mill Road in Kingston. The modern Sir John A. Macdonald Chapel, beside the cemetery office, features a dramatic stained glass window, commissioned in 1891 in memory of Sir John A. Installed in a tiny church at Redan, north of Brockville, the window was donated to the cemetery in 1980 when the chapel was built.

  His grave is marked by several plaques, all erected by the government of Canada: one marking his grave as that of a Father of Confederation, one as a Canadian prime minister, and a third as part of a program by Parks Canada to mark the gravesites of Canadian prime ministers. A simple stone cross marks his grave.

- A statue in City Park at the corner of West and King Street East in Kingston commemorates Sir John A.

- The town hall erected in 1856 at 124 John Street in nearby Napanee, Ontario, has been carefully preserved. Macdonald delivered his last campaign speech from its balcony in 1891.

Every year on June 6, the anniversary of Macdonald's death, the Kingston Historical Society organizes a memorial service in honour of Kingston's most famous son. For more information, visit www.heritagekingston.org.

• • • The Stanfield Football: Dropped Pass Sent PC Leader's Career for a Loss

A football mishandled by Conservative leader Robert Stanfield during the 1974 federal election campaign is possibly the most famous pigskin in Canadian history.

Those in the know say the dropped ball was among the factors that caused Stanfield to lose the election to Pierre Trudeau. Read on and see if you agree.

On May 30, 1974, Stanfield's DC-9 campaign airplane was flying from Halifax to Vancouver when it stopped for refuelling at North Bay, where the leader's campaign staff and the trailing press corps embarked onto the tarmac to stretch their legs.

With the RCMP and airport security watching closely, Brad Chapman, director of Stanfield's campaign tour operations, produced a football and began playing catch with members of the media.

"I had carried the football as a means of exercise for the weary press corps, having to sit long hours in airplanes, buses, and bars, with little chance to loosen up," recalls Chapman, who with colleague Peter Sharpe was looking after the needs and wants of the press.

Unknown to Chapman, Stanfield had also decided to go for a stroll around the aircraft. Seeing the football being tossed, he slipped out of his suit jacket and called for the ball. To the amazement of many, the leader began to throw thirty- and forty-yard perfect spiral passes to willing receivers.

"Occasionally, a receiver dropped the ball. And the ball was thrown back to the leader. Occasionally, he dropped the ball. Most of the time, though, like the press receivers, he caught the ball," recalls Chapman.

Meantime, Canadian Press photographer Doug Ball was snapping away with his camera. Before the plane took off en route to the west coast, his roll of film, which contained photos of Stanfield catching and dropping the ball, was shipped to Canadian Press's photo desk in Toronto.

"The rest is history," says Chapman.

The next day a Ball photo of Stanfield fumbling the football was on the front page of the *Globe and Mail* and other newspapers across Canada. "Political fumble?" said more than one newspaper caption that spring morning in 1974, when Stanfield's Conservatives were fighting to unseat Trudeau's minority Liberal government in an election forced by a non-confidence vote.

"The picture made him look really old," Don Sellar, who was covering the election for Southam News, was quoted as saying. "The long bony fingers, the ball slipping through. He looked terrible. And yet he didn't look terrible on the tarmac. ... He looked to be quite competent. He knew how to throw and catch: it's just that he dropped one."

Although the vote was still five weeks away, veteran Southam News reporter Charles Lynch told Ball, "Trudeau just won the election."

When the results were tallied on July 8, Canadians returned Trudeau to power with 141 seats, enough for a majority government. Stanfield's Conservatives won 95 ridings, 11 fewer than the party held when the election was called.

CP (Doug Ball)

This famous photograph helped knock Robert Stanfield out of the race for prime minister in 1973. The football, like Stanfield's bid to become prime minister, evaporated.

Few pundits blame the photo for Stanfield's defeat, but most say it played a role.

"It came at a particularly bad time, campaigning against Mr. Trudeau, who was perceived by the public as a very athletic guy — flips off diving boards and you name it," said Art Lyon, a lifelong Tory organizer who was working the campaign. "Then all of a sudden there's this one picture of a football and Mr. Stanfield, this crouched-over, bald guy in glasses. Put it this way: it didn't help."

Stanfield died in 2003 at the age of eighty-nine. The infamous football was kept by Chapman, but during the 1980s and 1990s, he went through several life transitions during which his personal goods were in storage, and somewhere along the way "the" football went missing.

"Some young fella might have chanced through my goods and, seeing an old football, thought he might put it to good use," Chapman speculates. "If it still exists, it's probably in pretty rugged condition. The last time I saw it in the 1980s, it had become pretty beat up. Like all good politicians, the ball has probably long since been recycled into anonymity."

WORTH NOTING...

Doug Ball, who took the famous Stanfield photograph and was rewarded with a National Newspaper Award for feature photography, joined the *Montreal Gazette* photo desk in 1984.

In the late 1980s he joined his friends, Trivial Pursuit co-inventors Chris Haney and Scott Abbott, to build two golf courses near Toronto, the Devil's Pulpit and the Devil's Paintbrush. Ball left the golf business in 1999, although he is still a member of the Devil's Pulpit Golf Association, which operates the two courses. Since then he has been a freelance photographer for a number of corporate clients, and in the fall of 2005 he published two coffee table books, *Life on a Press Pass*, with his brother Lynn, which includes photos the pair took over forty years as photographers in the media, and *The Greatest New Golf Courses in Canada* with writer John Gordon. *Life on a Press Pass* includes Doug's photos of Stanfield catching and dropping the football. Doug Ball lives in Oakville, Ontario.

IN CASE YOU WERE WONDERING...

Brad Chapman went on to a variety of other political posts following the 1974 campaign, including transportation director for Bill Davis's 1975 election campaign in Ontario, tour director for Michael Meighen's 1975 winning bid for the federal Tory Party presidency and for Jim Gillies's federal Tory leadership campaign in 1976, and tour operations director for the Joe Clark federal election campaigns of 1979 and 1980 and the Ontario Tory leadership campaign of Alan Pope in 1985.

In 1979 he was appointed chief of staff for John Fraser, minister of the environment and postmaster general of Canada. In 1987, he managed a Bay Street analyst's tour to Hong Kong, Beijing, Nanjing,

Shanghai, and Shenzhen. After a tour with Saskatchewan Trade and Investment as director of investment strategy and policy, in 1992 during a sweat lodge ceremony on the Little Big Horn River in Montana, Chapman was given the Crow Indian name of "Shamrock." Soon after, he served as director of public affairs for the late senator and Sawridge Band chief Walter P. Twinn.

In 1994, he managed the Juniper Lodge in Alberta, where he coordinated a spiritual wellness program. He now lives in Toronto, where he works in strategic investment banking, image marketing/consulting, and political history research and writing.

• • • Pierre Trudeau's Canoes and Buckskin Jacket: Paddling into History

Pierre Elliott Trudeau, Canada's fifteenth prime minister, evokes numerous images in the minds of Canadians: eloquent speaker in the House of Commons, always with the signature red rose in his lapel; charismatic and sexy political pop star who drove sports cars and dated famous women; and jokester who pirouetted behind Queen Elizabeth's back at Buckingham Palace.

Also etched in the memories of legions of Trudeau admirers is the image of the prime minister canoeing solo on a placid lake, often attired in his trademark buckskin jacket.

"He was the first prime minister to explore all three dimensions of the wild, wet part of Canada. He did this as an ocean surfer, a scuba diver, and as an accomplished canoe-tripper on several of the great rivers running into the Arctic Ocean," recalls Dr. Joseph MacInnis, Trudeau's friend for more than thirty years. "The canoe was one of his favourite ways of moving through the natural world. It took him to places that reflected the poetry of the nation he loved."

As a young boy, Trudeau trained himself at his family's summer cottage on Lac Tremblant in the Laurentian Mountains of Quebec to be a strong swimmer and canoeist. Friends say it was here that the vastness of Canada went into him and stayed with him forever.

Trudeau died on September 28, 2000, and is buried in the

Pierre Trudeau's buckskins, gloves, and a favourite paddle are lovingly cared for in a museum in Peterborough, Ontario, where two of his canoes are also on display.

Photo by Randy Ray

Trudeau family crypt at the St-Remi-de-Napierville Cemetery in Saint-Remi, Quebec.

His buckskin jacket, a pair of beaded buckskin gloves, two of his canoes, and a paddle, all on loan from the estate of Pierre Elliot Trudeau, are part of the collection at the Canadian Canoe Museum in Peterborough, Ontario, which bills itself as "home of the world's largest collection of canoes and kayaks."

The Trudeau artifacts are by far the most popular items in the museum, says collection manager Kim Watson.

The high-collared jacket, with buttons of antler and decorative red and green beading adorning the right arm, chest, and pockets, was commissioned by the chamber of commerce in Maniwaki, Quebec, after Trudeau visited Maniwaki shortly after becoming prime minister and expressed interest in Algonquin culture. The gloves were also commissioned by the chamber of commerce.

A paddle displayed in a humidity-controlled case that also contains the gloves and jacket was made by the Peterborough Canoe Company. Trudeau often used it when he paddled on lakes in the Gatineau Hills near Ottawa.

Two of Trudeau's canoes hang from the ceiling inside the museum. One is made of birch bark and was built by Patrick Maranda of Lac Rapide, Quebec, circa 1968, and commissioned by the Maniwaki Chamber of Commerce. The other is a canvas-covered canoe made by the Chestnut Canoe Company and paddled by Trudeau when he was a young man, says information provided by the museum.

On the bow of the canvas canoe is the name *CA IRA*, which means "it goes."

For more information, visit www.canoemuseum.net or call (705) 748-9153.

SPORTS
• • •
Beyond the Finish Line

• • • David Bailey: Cracking the Four-Minute Mile

When David Bailey crossed the finish line of a mile race at a track meet in San Diego on June 11, 1966, his first reaction was "Crap, I missed it again."

The "it" was the four-minute mile, which up to that time had not been broken by any Canadian runner. Bailey, who was a University of Toronto pharmacy student at the time, had run just over 4:01 in the past, and he knew "by the third quarter [of the race] that we were in great shape" to better four minutes. But he felt that in this race he ran his last two hundred yards a bit flat and hadn't done enough to crack the famous barrier.

But good friend and world-class half-miler Bill Crothers was at the finish line with a stopwatch and told Bailey he'd done it. Bailey's time of 3:59.1 marked the first time a Canadian had broken four minutes, and with that race he took his place among this country's sports icons. Sitting on the back deck of his London, Ontario, home, Bailey reminisced about that momentous race some forty years ago. "I was absolutely thrilled," he said of his historic run. "I remember feeling extremely exhausted and my legs were like rubber. Then we had to jog back to the hotel."

Since the late 1950s the Canadian sports media had been calling on homegrown track athletes to break the four-minute barrier, a feat first achieved by Roger Bannister of Britain in 1954. But they had to wait for Bailey's 1966 run in California. When he flew home via Chicago, he was surprised to see his mother at the airport there. The *Toronto Star* had flown her to Chicago to meet him and to get an exclusive interview before he arrived in Canada.

But Bailey, who was a member of the East York Track Club along with Crothers and Bruce Kidd, wasn't finished. A year later in July at Toronto's Varsity Stadium, before thousands of screaming fans, Bailey shattered his personal best with a time of 3:57.7, becoming the first Canadian to run a mile under four minutes on Canadian soil. It was also a Canadian record that stood for a decade. For Bailey, that race was the ultimate of his track career. "I was absolutely exhausted, but I said to myself now I know what it's like to have [thousands of] people in the palm of your hand."

Though he competed until 1978, Bailey, who lost his right eye in an accident when he was nine years old, would never again crack the four-minute barrier, despite running 4:02 or better about twenty times. But for Bailey, track was not his life plan; it was a means to an end.

What happened to Bailey after those heady days among track's elite? He got his master's degree and then his PhD in pharmacology, coaching track and raising a family along the way with his wife, Barbara. In the 1980s, he did drug research for a private firm in Toronto before getting an

Photo by Mark Kearney

opportunity to pursue his work in London in 1986. Today, he's busy with clinical pharmacology research at the London Health Sciences Centre.

Throughout his career, Bailey has made his name even more famous internationally with groundbreaking research. If you've ever taken drugs that warn of the dangers of doing so with grapefruit juice, you can thank Bailey. Until his work, no one had paid much attention to the fact that food, and specifically grapefruit juice,

David Bailey, seen here in a 2005 photo, fondly remembers the day he cracked the four-minute mile barrier.

could interact with drugs and have significantly bad side effects. "It changed the whole thinking of natural products and drug interactions," he says.

These days Bailey still gets "a real kick" out of the research he does, but now in his early sixties he has no plans to do any kind of competitive running even at the masters level. "I've run hundreds of races and people say 'why don't you run another race?' I say 'I left it all on the track. I have nothing left to give.'"

• • • Marilyn Bell: Lady of the Lake

Though she will always be remembered as the teenager who was the first to conquer Lake Ontario back in 1954, Marilyn Bell never planned on swimming all the way across.

The then sixteen-year-old expected only to challenge famed American long-distance swimmer Florence Chadwick, who had been offered $10,000 to attempt the crossing. "I did not think I could do it," Bell says now from her New Jersey home, "but I didn't think Florence Chadwick could do it either." In fact, the Toronto teen planned "to go as far as [Chadwick] went and then go a little bit further to prove a Canadian could go farther than the American."

But as many Canadians know, Bell did much more than just go "a little bit further" than Chadwick. When she finished crossing the lake after more than twenty hours of swimming, Marilyn Bell became a household name across the country and created a media frenzy that still reverberates today.

In fact, Bell, who has lived in New Jersey ever since marrying her husband, Joe Di Lascio, in 1957, says she's amazed not only that people from that era still talk about her historic swim but that children today even know about it. When she was in Toronto in 2004 to officially open the Canadian National Exhibition, it was "mind boggling" to her that young children were there to greet and applaud her.

But her swim across Lake Ontario has become something of an iconic moment in Canadian sports history. The young girl was the toast of the country and won the Lou Marsh Trophy later that year as Canada's best female athlete. She remembers going from a shy girl who was more of a follower to someone who was expected to attend banquets, make speeches, and handle reporters' questions on almost a daily basis. She must have done something right because she recalls how "Canadians poured their hearts out to me."

Bell didn't start swimming until she was nine years old, and by her own admission she "didn't come first very often" in competitions. Once she switched over to longer races under the watchful eye of coach Gus Ryder, she began to blossom. She swam and won the ladies' marathon race around Absicon Island in Atlantic City in 1954 and knew she could handle long distances.

But no one had ever successfully crossed Lake Ontario, and the thought had never entered her mind that she could be the first. It was Ryder who planted the idea of challenging Chadwick in the race, but little attention was paid to the young Canadian. The way the event was set up, Bell had to start her swim at night on the American side and hope that her boat, with Ryder and others in it, would find her. "I dove in thinking 'where am I going?' That was really scary."

But she and the boat linked up, and the teenager, who says she's always been afraid of fish, began stroking through the turbulent waters. She remembers feeling better when the sun rose that morning, and Ryder encouraged her by writing messages on a chalkboard as she made her way to the Canadian shore. "There were lots of times when I was ready to give up," she says, but she didn't want to let down the coach who believed in her.

As she neared the shore she mostly remembers chaos. "I was so exhausted and very confused at the end," she says, noting that it was a good hour before she realized she had conquered the lake. The following year she successfully swam across the English Channel, but it was a different feeling from that of her historic Canadian swim. "When I went into Lake Ontario I was the underdog; no one expected anything." But in 1955, the whole country assumed she'd swim the channel.

The years since she stopped marathon swimming have been good to Bell. She had children and grandchildren, earned her BA, and was a teacher in New Jersey for some twenty years. She had to become an American citizen to teach and recalls that career with great fondness. Though Bell says

Courtesy of Marilyn Bell

Marilyn Bell will always be remembered for her historic 1954 swim across Lake Ontario.

she loved her "wonderful" swimming career, "the best part of my life came later."

Her background as a teacher surfaced one year at a banquet when Wayne Gretzky was honoured as Canadian athlete of the year. She and the hockey star didn't say much at first until he told her that when he was in school he picked her as the subject for an essay on famous Canadians. Being a teacher, the first words out of her mouth were "What kind of grade did you get on it?" she recalls with a laugh.

A back injury forced Bell to give up swimming a few years ago, but she does enjoy water therapy at a facility where no one knows of her past exploits. "They do marvel at how well I can float," she says. She's an active volunteer in her community and tries to visit Canada as often as possible.

"I'm still a Canadian at heart," she says. "It's always going home for me. I'm always really happy to go over the border."

Photo by Ken Jeffries

Big Ben and rider Ian Millar are commemorated by this statue in Perth, Ontario. The prized horse died in 1999; Millar continues to ride. (See story at right.)

• • • Big Ben and Ian Millar

Big Ben, originally named Winston, after British Prime Minister Winston Churchill, came to Canada in 1983 from the Hooydonk Farm in northern Belgium. His owner, equestrian Ian Millar, purchased and brought the 17.3-hand chestnut to Millar Brooke Farm in Perth, Ontario.

In 1984, Big Ben started competing in show jumping events with Millar in the saddle. The pair made a glorious tandem, with forty Grand Prix victories, the World Show Jumping Championship two years in a row, and $1.5 million in prize money.

In 1994 Big Ben retired to the Millar Brooke Farm. He was the second horse inducted into the Ontario Sports Legends Hall of Fame (Northern Dancer was the first) and in 1999 was honoured by Canada Post with a stamp.

At the age of twenty-three, Big Ben was euthanized at Millar's farm on December 11, 1999, after veterinarians said nothing could be done to ease suffering caused by a persistent case of equine colic. He was buried on a knoll overlooking the farm.

On May 22, 2005, a full-size bronze sculpture of Big Ben and Millar by sculptor Steward Smith was unveiled in Perth at the corner of Wilson and Herriott streets, overlooking Stewart Park.

Millar, a native of Halifax and an eight-time Olympian and show jumping legend, was named to the Order of Canada in 1986. He continues to run his farm and also spends time in Florida, where he shows horses. He competes in as many as twenty-five show jumping events a year.

Canada Post stamp celebrating Big Ben and rider Ian Millar, one of Canada's sporting dynamic duos.

• • • Betsy Clifford: Champion Downhill Skier

Betsy Clifford will never forget her second-place finish in the World Downhill Skiing Championship in 1974 at St. Moritz, Switzerland. "I was neck-in-neck with Annemarie Moser-Proell of Austria," she recalls. "It came down to one turn and I lost by 2/100ths of a second. There was nothing I could have done better ... it was a great race."

While she lost by the slimmest of margins, Clifford, a native of Old Chelsea, Quebec, just north of Ottawa, still managed to bring home a silver medal to add to a string of honours she would win after learning to ski in the Gatineau Hills of southwestern Quebec at age three.

In 1968, at the age of fourteen, Clifford became the youngest Canadian skier ever to compete at the Olympics. In 1970, in Val Gardena, Italy, she became the youngest skier to win a medal at the World Championships when she earned gold in the giant slalom; she was named most newsworthy woman in sports in 1971 after winning the special slalom in Schruns, Austria, and the slalom in Val D'Isere, France, to finish second in overall Slalom World Cup standings.

In 1972, she broke both heels while training for a World Cup race at Grindelwald, Switzerland, and vowed to retire. The accident forced her to miss the 1972 Olympics. In 1973, she returned to competitive ski racing and dominated the Can-Am series with five victories, finishing seventy-two points ahead of her nearest competitor.

Courtesy of Canadian Ski Museum

Betsy Clifford demonstrates her championship style.

Now in her early fifties, she is a member of Canada's Sports Hall of Fame and the American National Ski Hall of Fame.

Clifford has married for a second time and lives in Lanark, Ontario, a town seventy kilometres west of Ottawa. She's a certified Level 3 ski instructor and has worked as a ski patroller at nearby Mount Pakenham, which was developed by her late father, John Clifford, and is currently owned by her sister Joanne.

Clifford, whose married name is Whitehall, has worked for the federal government since 1981. In 2006 she was working in human resources with the Department of Fisheries and Oceans, Canadian Coast Guard section.

The bib and Rossignol skis she was wearing in Val Gardena in 1970 when she won the gold medal are in the collection of the Canadian Ski Museum in Ottawa.

For more information, visit www.skimuseum.ca.

WORTH NOTING...

Clifford's late father, John, was often referred to as a ski pioneer and "the father of popular skiing." The Ottawa native spent seven decades as a racer, ski centre developer, instructor, and ski resort owner. He is credited with bringing snowmaking technology to Canada in the mid-1950s, adding nearly two months to the downhill ski season each year. "Thanks to John, people now ski into mid-April until they are bored and want to play golf," says his long-time friend Keith Nesbitt. Clifford passed away in 2002 in Almonte, Ontario, at the age of seventy-nine.

• • • Ron Ellis: Mr. Dependable

If there has ever been a winger who gave his all at both ends of the ice, while rarely being caught out of position, it's Ron Ellis.

"Under coach Punch Imlach, it was not a good idea to wander off of your wing. If you did, you might be watching the rest of the game from the end of the bench," says Ellis.

Ellis was born on January 8, 1945, in Lindsay, Ontario, northeast of Toronto, and played his minor hockey mostly in Toronto and Ottawa. When he was fourteen and attending high school in Ottawa, Toronto Maple Leafs coach Punch Imlach and general manager King Clancy visited his home and asked him to join the Toronto Marlboroughs junior hockey organization the following season.

He developed into a pro prospect and led the Marlies in goals during his Memorial Cup–winning year in 1963–64. He joined the Leafs in 1964, scoring twenty-three goals and narrowly losing the Calder Trophy for rookie of the year to Detroit Red Wings netminder Roger Crozier. Ellis spent his entire career with the Leafs and retired in 1980 after playing in 1,034 games and notching 332 goals and 308 assists.

In game six of the Stanley Cup finals in 1967, Ellis provided the crucial first goal to help the Leafs win the game 3–1 and take the cup. In the 1972 Canada–Russia Summit Series, the five-foot-nine, 190-pounder was a member of the Team Canada squad that beat the Russians on Paul Henderson's dramatic goal with only seconds remaining in the final game. He was on a line with Henderson and Bobby Clarke.

After retiring from pro hockey, Ellis worked in the

Courtesy of Ron Ellis

Ron Ellis is still involved in hockey with the Hockey Hall of Fame in Toronto.

Toronto area as a teacher and in the insurance business and ran his own sporting goods store for six years. In 1993, he joined the Hockey Hall of Fame, where he is the director of public affairs and assistant to the president.

He supports the work of Christian Athletic Ministries and lives in Caledon East near Toronto with his wife, Jan.

WORTH NOTING...

Prior to the 1968–69 season, former Maple Leafs great Irvine "Ace" Bailey insisted that Ellis wear his retired No. 6 because he admired his high-calibre yet clean style of play. Ellis's father, Randy, played with the Toronto Marlboroughs under Harold Ballard, coach of the team at the time and later owner of the Leafs.

• • • Our First Gold Medal: Still a Mystery

George Orton of Strathroy, Ontario, was a premier track athlete in Canada and beyond during the 1890s. But when he entered the 1900 Olympic Games in Paris, France, he was representing his American university team. Canada did not send an official team to the Olympics until 1904, which left Orton with the only option of competing for his adopted home south of the border.

Orton, who had previously attended the University of Toronto, later became a successful runner at the University of Pennsylvania, where he was working on his graduate degree. Although he received his PhD in 1896, he remained an active athlete, and apparently his mile time of 4:21.8 stood as a Canadian record for thirty years. At the Paris Olympics, Orton won a gold medal in the 2,500-metre steeplechase and a bronze in the 400-metre hurdles.

But whatever happened to those historic medals? Officials at Canada's Sports Hall of Fame would like to know because they don't have them. The local museum in Orton's hometown of Strathroy is interested in finding them too. We contacted the International Centre for Olympic Studies at the University of Western Ontario in London, Ontario, and the University of Pennsylvania's athletic department, but they didn't know either.

An archivist at the University of Pennsylvania emailed to say there are about forty to fifty items about Orton in the U. Penn. collection, but "we do not know the location of his Olympic medals." She indicated, however, that more research was being conducted into Orton's life. In the meantime, this is what she knows: Orton won national titles in Canada, the U.S., and the United Kingdom at various race lengths. He was also an outstanding athlete in other sports, playing soccer in Philadelphia and starting the hockey team at the university.

Orton was a teacher and a track coach and taught languages at various educational academies. He also founded two New Hampshire camps, Camp Tecumseh in 1902 and Camp Iroquois in 1916. Before the First World War, Orton was a co-author of *A History of Athletics in Pennsylvania* in several volumes. From 1928 to 1934 he was director of Philadelphia's Municipal Stadium.

From 1941 until his death June 25, 1958, he made his home with his step-daughter, Doris B. Bolton, in Center Harbor, New Hampshire. Although we contacted the nearby Meredith Historical Society, Camp Tecumseh, town officials in Center Harbor, and the historical society there, no one had information about what happened to those medals. Perhaps there are relatives who know, but we were unable to contact any descendants.

So, for now, the mystery of where Orton's medals are remains. If any reader knows of their whereabouts or has leads that might help us solve the riddle, please contact us. It's one hurdle we'd like to clear.

• • • The Great One's Hockey Card: The Holy Grail

A hockey card showing Wayne Gretzky in an Edmonton Oilers uniform during his first season in the National Hockey League is known among collectors as "the holy grail of hockey cards."

And for good reason: it's worth enough to cover the down payment on a good-sized home.

At a public auction in August 2005, the Gretzky rookie card, which was printed in 1979 by Canadian card manufacturer O-Pee-Chee, fetched $75,594 (US$62,374). It's the highest price ever paid for a hockey card. O-Pee-Chee Gretzky rookie cards in top condition usually sell at most for $1,500. The card was sold by Illinois-based consignment auction house MastroNet.

Joe Orlando, president of Santa Ana, California–based PSA and PSA/DNA Authentication Services, said it was the "finest example" of a Gretzky rookie card the company has seen in its fifteen-year history.

It scored the best rating possible — in collectors' lingo known as "PSA Gem Mint 10" — based on the strength of its corners and the centering and quality of the photograph of No. 99, who dominated score sheets in the NHL between 1979 and 1999.

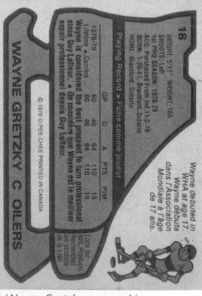

Canada's most valuable sports card shows Wayne Gretzky as a rookie.

A number of the 9 million cards the company has rated since 1991 have received the coveted PSA Gem Mint 10. However, the Gretzky card sold by MastroNet is the first of 1,740 O-Pee-Chee Gretzky rookie cards assessed by PSA and PSA/DNA Authentication Services to earn such a high rating, said Orlando.

"Many factors contributed to the interest in the card," he said. "Gretzky is, of course, considered the greatest hockey player in history and there is great demand for key rookie cards in all sports. The O-Pee-Chee card is an extremely difficult card to find in PSA Mint 9 or better condition ... there is always a market for the best of the best material and, so far, no other Gretzky rookie card has been able to match this fine example."

During a twenty-year career with the Oilers, Los Angeles Kings, St. Louis Blues, and New York Rangers, Gretzky scored 2,857 points in 1,487 regular season games, won more than two dozen awards, set numerous records, and led the Oilers to four Stanley Cups.

For security reasons, the person who won the bidding for the Gretzky card asked for anonymity, but we can tell you the owner is an American living on the U.S. east coast.

• • • Anne Heggtveit:
The Barbara Ann Scott of Skiing

Heading into the 1960 Winter Olympics in Squaw Valley, California, Canadian Anne Heggtveit was considered the woman to beat in slalom skiing. But her Olympic story almost ended in tragedy before the Games even got started.

Training in Switzerland before the Olympics, Heggtveit was rushing down a mountain while workers were busy packing snow on the trails. When she was about halfway down the hill, a man working near the slopes to her left hit her in the leg with his snow shovel. She didn't fall, but she sensed something was wrong.

"I thought he'd broken my leg," Heggtveit recalls more than forty-five years later. But she made it to the bottom and was able to put weight on her leg. She had lunch and was getting ready to head back to train when she noticed her leg was bleeding. The shovel had cut into her tibia but had fortunately not severed a muscle. "That would have been disastrous."

Despite the setback, Heggtveit kept her eyes on the prize, something she had dreamed of since she was a child — to be the first Canadian to win a gold medal in her sport and become the Barbara Ann Scott of skiing.

The parallels between her and the 1948 Olympic skating champion were certainly there. Like Scott, Heggtveit had grown up in the Ottawa area, learning to ski at Rockliffe Park at the age of two. She started

Courtesy of Anne Heggtveit-Hamilton

Despite a leg injury, Anne Heggtveit skied brilliantly to win Olympic gold in the slalom in 1960.

competing young too, and was winning races before she was ten. By age fourteen, Heggtveit was competing and winning ski competitions in Europe. Her father had been a champion cross-country skier and her uncles were also accomplished athletes, so Heggtveit was raised with the attitude that she could be a world-beater.

A broken leg in 1955 hampered her chances for a medal at the 1956 Olympics, but she was inspired by fellow Canadian Lucille Wheeler who won bronze there. Although Heggtveit didn't reach the podium in the downhill or the giant slalom in the 1960 Games, her focus had always been on the slalom.

Standing at the starting gate for that event, she had a good feeling about her chances, she recalls. "I felt really good and confident. Funny when I look at the film of that I look very nervous, but I didn't feel nervous."

Her first run was a gem, and the time she set held up by the end of the event, winning her the gold. In fact, her margin of victory is still the largest among any skiers in Olympic slalom history. But as she sits in her Vermont home in 2006, Heggtveit mentions a bit of overlooked sporting trivia. She was also the winner of the combined skiing event, but in those days the Olympics didn't recognize that with a medal. The International Ski Federation did, however, so Heggtveit actually walked away from those Olympics with another gold medal. "It annoys me that people won't give me credit for the two gold medals."

But despite that, she, like her hero Scott from twelve years before, was the toast of Canada upon her return. Just as Scott did, Heggtveit received a ticker tape parade in Ottawa ("It was quite a homecoming") and that year won the Lou Marsh Trophy as Canada's outstanding athlete, beating out a young Russ Jackson of the Ottawa Rough Riders.

She had a couple of hills named for her, one in the Blue Mountain area of Collingwood, Ontario, and another at Camp Fortune in Quebec's Gatineau Hills, about twenty kilometres north of Ottawa. To this day, she's never seen the former and never skied the latter.

Winning the gold was how she capped her career. Once she'd achieved her lifelong goal, Heggtveit was "quite happy to pack it in." She'd seen one of her teammates die a couple of years before and knew all about injuries that plague people in the sport. "You start thinking about things like that as you get older," she says.

She did very little skiing for the next several years, but once her two children got interested, she began hitting the slopes of Quebec, where she lived for a while and worked as an instructor for Learn to Ski programs. In 1979, she and her husband Ross Hamilton moved to Vermont on Lake Champlain but not near the slopes. Heggtveit worked in accounting until 2000, and has since started her own photography and floral design company. Heggtveit says her knees "aren't good" these days, but she still skis occasionally if the weather and conditions are favourable.

She believes her win in 1960 helped inspire other Canadians, notably 1968 Olympic champion Nancy Greene, and she continues to watch her native country's athletes during the Olympics and in other events. Heggtveit says she thinks about her gold medal only around Olympic Games time, when media contact her for interviews, but she looks back on the glorious moment in 1960 on the podium as "pretty exciting."

• • • The Henderson Puck: The Puck Stops Where?

In the hockey world, it's taken on almost mythical status — the most prized souvenir from what many consider the greatest hockey tournament of all time.

It was 1972, Canada versus the Soviet Union — a series that wasn't just about two countries but one with political overtones, East versus West.

The Soviets dazzled the world and stunned the Canadians with their sharp passing, smooth skating, and ability to score quickly. The Canadians, down but never out, doggedly plodded their way back into the series and in the final game, on September 28, Paul Henderson scored the most famous goal in hockey history to give Canada the slim 6–5 victory.

His goal, at the 19:26 mark of the third period, won the eight-game series for Canada.

But unlike most goal scorers, Henderson didn't retrieve the instantly famous puck that sealed the win. For a long time, fans wondered — what happened to that puck?

There were plenty of rumours, and they almost all led to Team Canada defenceman Pat Stapleton, known for collecting hockey memorabilia. But if Stapleton had the puck he wasn't admitting it — that is, until it was shown clearly on video from the game that he had retrieved it.

Stapleton remained coy, playing down the puck's significance when the media called, never letting on just what he had done with it. He once said in an interview that he wasn't even sure where he'd put it. "What I want to do is skate with it with my grandchildren on the pond. What we'll do is skate around for a while and then shoot it into a snow bank. And that'll be it."

But that wasn't it. Eventually the story surfaced that he'd passed on the puck to his good friend and fellow defenceman from that series, Bill White. Why give it to him? These days, White laughs at the question, saying that Stapleton did it to turn inquirers onto White. "It takes the pressure off him, and I start getting all the calls," he says.

Today, the two of them will say only that the puck "is in a safe place" somewhere in Ontario, and they have no plans for doing anything with it. "The status of that puck will never change," White said from his office in Woodbridge, Ontario, where he does work quoting on jobs for York

West Plumbing Supplies. "We never disclose where it is because it takes the pressure off each one of us."

"That was the puck used in the last thirty-some seconds. Why I [picked up the puck] I don't know. Maybe I shouldn't have," Stapleton, who is retired in Strathroy, Ontario, adds with a laugh. "I don't know what people expect of the puck. It's a puck. There were no special markings on it."

There have been a couple of suggestions as to what to do with it: auction the puck off to the highest bidder, for example, or put it in the Hockey Hall of Fame. Some have suggested that if it's sold a portion of the proceeds should be given to some of the Russian hockey players from that series who are scraping by on low incomes. However, there are concerns that there is no guarantee the money would ever reach the Russian players or that it shouldn't be Canadian hockey players' responsibility. "I just don't know what to do," White adds.

Henderson has never approached them asking for the puck, but he has suggested that it should go to the Hockey Hall of Fame. Stapleton says the players from the 1972 series have joked from time to time about the puck's significance. "It belongs to all of the guys," Stapleton said in an interview from his home. "It belongs to Canada."

Courtesy of The Leadership Group

Paul Henderson is still a popular draw on the speaker circuit, but the puck that made him famous is hidden away in a secret location.

To that end, if the puck does surface it would be a good idea to take it on a tour of Canada with other memorabilia from that series, says Ed Gryschuk of Ficel Marketing Corp., which is expected to handle the publicity if the two hockey players ever reveal the puck's whereabouts. Noting that both White and Stapleton are renowned for telling "lots of stories" about the puck, Gryschuk says he's heard the price tag for such an artifact could be anywhere from $100,000 to $1 million.

Stapleton says he is asked about the puck all the time, and that the series lives on because baby boomers remember it fondly. Students today regularly do school projects on the Canada–Soviet games. "It was a tremendously rewarding experience," says Stapleton of the series. "How do you know going into something like that that it would remain part of the folklore?"

A CBC-TV dramatization of the series broadcast in spring 2006 added to the prominence of the 1972 games, what White calls "a mini-war on ice." Says Stapleton, "It was society against society."

As for what might happen to the puck, it seems like it's anyone's guess for now. "I have no idea," says White of the possible price it might fetch. "I imagine it would go to a real select group." Stapleton also doesn't speculate but knows it would be a popular item. "It's the mystery of it, I guess."

● ●

Henderson Still Scoring Spiritually

Henderson has certainly not forgotten that series, as people ask him regularly about the goal or praise him for scoring it. "It's all win-win. I never tire of it," he told us in an interview. As for not picking up the puck when he scored, Henderson said, "The last thing I thought of was getting that puck" because there was such joy and pandemonium following his goal. "I never gave it one iota of thought."

As a frequent public speaker, Henderson, a native of Kincardine, Ontario, has rarely been out of the limelight since the 1972 series. For the past twenty-one years he's been the head of the Leadership Group, a Mississauga-based organization that provides counselling and spiritual guidance for men. It's a non-denominational Christian group that deals with people throughout parts of southern Ontario and Quebec. The group is also setting up in such places as Calgary and Winnipeg.

Twenty-five years after scoring his goal, Henderson became the first living Canadian to be honoured with his likeness on a postage stamp when Canada Post released a tribute stamp in 1997.

● ●

• • • George Hungerford and Roger Jackson: Underdog Oarsmen

In the sporting pantheon of underdogs, few overcame the odds as much as rowers George Hungerford and Roger Jackson did.

The two Canadians, who started rowing as a pair only about a month before the 1964 Olympics, went to the Tokyo Games with virtually no expectations other than trying to do their best under the circumstances. It was certainly not the kind of preparation a typical Olympic athlete would follow, which is why the duo's emergence as gold medallists caught everyone, including themselves, off guard.

Both young men were rowers in Vancouver, Hungerford as part of the eights crew and Jackson in the pairs. But Hungerford suffered a bout of mononucleosis in 1964 that sapped him of his energy and put him in bed for about five weeks. It appeared his Olympic dream was over when officials substituted a spare rower in his place. Meanwhile, Jackson lost his partner, which left him up the creek without a paddle.

Hungerford managed to recover with some time to spare before the Tokyo Games, and he and Jackson were asked to pair up to see if they worked well together. The coaches told them they could go to the Olympics if the pairing was successful; their goal would be "not to embarrass Canada."

The two determined individuals decided to give it a try, even though most pairs racers at that level would normally work together for months or years to perfect their teamwork, Hungerford says. "Our challenge was to come together as pair in every respect." Pairs racing requires the team to have a sensitive relationship that involves being matched well physically and mentally, and having so little time to work all that out was a huge task. "It wasn't easy for Roger and it wasn't easy for me either. The pair is a very temperamental boat," Hungerford recalls.

Despite the obvious challenges they faced, the two were impressive enough early on that they got their wish to compete at the Games. But while other world-class rowers were preparing mentally before the heats, Jackson and Hungerford were still practising basic physical skills that their competitors would have long ago ironed out.

What worked in the duo's favour was that few had expectations for them, and they trained with no media scrutiny. Nevertheless, Hungerford and Jackson overcame the odds and ended up with the fastest times in the heats.

Even still, when it came to the final, the Germans and the Dutch were expected to end up on top, but Hungerford remembers that with only a few other competitors to beat to get a medal the two Canadians thought "why not?" Their strategy was to go out hard and fast for the first two-thirds of the course and hope that Hungerford, who was still recovering, could hold on. Their first twenty-five strokes of the race "were almost perfect," says Hungerford, and the pair took the lead. They knew they had to keep pushing just to hang on, but the Dutch were closing fast. Hungerford recalls that at the end "my gas tank was empty; I'd given everything I could." But the Canadians held on for gold.

Hungerford says all of Canada was stunned by the victory, and he and Jackson weren't even interviewed by Canadian media until well after the race because the reporters had been at the main stadium watching sprinter Harry Jerome. But the duo's story and victory certainly became well appreciated shortly thereafter; Jackson and Hungerford shared the Lou Marsh Trophy as Canada's athletes of the year in 1964.

The two rowed together for another year, but illness slowed Hungerford again. Hungerford went on to study law and has worked as a lawyer ever since, most recently with the firm Fasken Martineau DuMoulin in Vancouver. He has been a governor and chairman of the Bristish Columbia division of the Olympic Trust of Canada and was a chairman of the B.C. Sports Hall of Fame for four years.

Jackson became a respected academic in the sports world and one of the leaders in the Olympic Games movement. A former director of Sport Canada, Jackson served three terms as president of the Canadian Olympic Committee and was dean of the Faculty of Kinesiology at the University of Calgary from 1978 to 1988. In 2004 he formed Roger Jackson & Associates Ltd., a private consulting practice that has seen him work on six Olympic bids, including Great Britain's successful bid for the 2012 Summer Games.

He is the chief executive officer of the Own the Podium 2010 project for the Winter Olympics in British Columbia, a $110-million sport technical initiative designed to help Canada win more medals at the 2010 Games than any other nation and place in the top three overall at the 2010 Paralympic Winter Games.

Both Jackson and Hungerford are members of the Canada Sports Hall of Fame and have received the Order of Canada.

Looking back at that 1964 victory, Hungerford says it gave him the confidence in life to tackle just about anything, including participation in the many community projects for which he is well known in Vancouver, such as the new rowing centre there. He and Jackson remain good friends. Hungerford says the gold medal was "an experience that was a fantastic journey. It shaped my life."

• • • Russ Jackson: The All-Canadian Quarterback

No one wants to see a homegrown quarterback shine in the Canadian Football League more than Russ Jackson — if only because it'll mean people will stop asking him about the issue.

There are many reasons why it hasn't happened in recent decades, says Jackson, but if it ever does happen "he's going to have to be someone really special."

Someone like Jackson. In a brilliant career that saw him lead the Ottawa Rough Riders to three Grey Cup victories, Jackson set the standard, not only for Canadian-born quarterbacks, but for quarterbacks period.

The Hamilton, Ontario, native won three Most Outstanding Player awards, something unprecedented for a homegrown player in the CFL. Given that he started with the Rough Riders in 1958 as defensive back, Jackson's accomplishments were all the more unexpected. "At that time to think you might make it as a Canadian quarterback was unheard of," Jackson said in an interview from his home in Burlington, Ontario, near Hamilton.

But when two other quarterbacks got injured, Jackson got his chance and proved that being a Canadian at that position was no handicap. But since he retired from the game in 1969, there have been few Canadians who've been given the chance to play quarterback. Jackson, however, helped Ottawa to a Grey Cup win in 1960 and led the team to victory again in 1968 and 1969. He picked up his Most Outstanding Player awards at intervals along the way, which he recalls with pride: "winning it over a period of time because you maintained a degree of excellence" was satisfying, he says.

Jackson saved his best for 1969, the year he announced he would be

Once Russ Jackson got his chance to play quarterback for the Ottawa Rough Riders, he became one of the all-time great pivots.

Courtesy of Canadian Football Hall of Fame and Museum

retiring. He enjoyed a stellar season, including a playoff victory over the Toronto Argonauts, whose coach Leo Cahill had claimed it "would take an act of God" for his team to lose to Ottawa after the Argos won the first of a two-game total points playoff. Jackson responded with a memorable performance that saw his team trounce the Argos 32–3 and win the series 46–25. Ottawa then defeated Saskatchewan in the Grey Cup. "To go through that year and end on a high note, that had to make it special," Jackson recalls.

The quarterback stuck to his word, though, and said farewell to the game. He had been a teacher and vice-principal during his playing days but wanted to be a principal and believed he could do that only away from football. He became principal of an Ottawa high school soon afterward and held that position in different schools in both Ottawa and the Peel Region of Ontario until his retirement in 1992.

He also did a stint as a CFL colour commentator with the CBC in the 1970s and tried coaching for a couple of years in the middle of that decade with the Argonauts. Coaching wasn't a successful fit for Jackson and he was let go from the team in 1976. He enjoy the commentating, however, noting it was far less stressful than coaching ever was. But of the Argo job, he now says that while it was upsetting at the time, "I'm glad I tried it."

Jackson speaks more enthusiastically of his years as a principal, during which he helped one high school make the transition from being English to unilingual French, saved some programs at another, and helped a new school in Peel get started. "There was always something neat about the schools I was at," he says.

Jackson coached basketball during his years as an educator and occasionally helped mentor some high school quarterbacks, but when he stepped down, he says, "It was time, I was ready. It was like football."

He did some colour commentating for Hamilton Tiger-Cats games after that and still attends their home games. Ever the quarterback, Jackson watches the action on the field trying to analyze what the defence might do on a particular down. "I enjoy watching the game from the aspect of being the quarterback. It's kind of fun for me that way."

Since moving to Burlington about six years ago, Jackson has kept busy playing golf at nearby Credit Valley Golf & Country Club, skiing in the winter, and doing a great deal of charity work, including raising funds for the football program of his alma mater, McMaster University. He's still an avid fan of the CFL and thinks the players are better trained and better coached than in his day. Fans still recognize him just about everywhere he goes, and he's happy to answer questions and talk about the game. "And they recognize my voice which is always interesting."

As for the quarterbacks that came after him, Jackson believes there were many good ones but that Doug Flutie in particular stood out. "He had that leadership that made him special. He made good teams into great teams. That's what a quarterback can do."

Not unlike Russ Jackson.

• • • Garry Monahan: Drafted First

As professional hockey players go, Garry Monahan was never a household name. But when he was selected by the Montreal Canadiens in the National Hockey League entry draft in 1963, he became a part of hockey history.

Monahan, who was born on October 20, 1946, was the first player picked in the first ever National Hockey League draft of amateur players seventeen years of age and older.

The Barrie, Ontario, native, best known as a defensive forward in the NHL, played junior hockey with the St. Michael's College organization, which has spawned many hockey greats, including Joe Primeau, Dave Keon, Red Kelly, Frank Mahovlich, and Eric Lindros.

He also skated for the Peterborough Petes and minor league teams in Houston and Cleveland before jumping to the NHL, where he played for the Canadiens, Detroit Red Wings, Los Angeles Kings, Vancouver Canucks, and Toronto Maple Leafs.

Courtesy of Garry Monahan

During his twelve-year career, Monahan played in 748 regular season games and scored 116 goals and 169 assists. After retiring from the NHL in 1979 he played amateur hockey in Japan for three years with the Seibu Bears.

Monahan became a real estate agent in 1990. He lives in West Vancouver, where he is an agent with Royal LePage Garry Monahan Realty Ltd.

After staying off skates for twenty years, he tied up the blades in 2003 as a member of the Canucks alumni. He also

Historic draft pick Garry Monahan has traded his blades for a career in real estate.

plays golf and tennis and spends many winter weekends skiing at Whistler.

WORTH NOTING...

The second player taken in the 1963 draft was Peter Mahovlich, who later joined the Detroit Red Wings. Coincidentally, about three years into their careers, the two swapped teams, with Monahan going to Detroit and Mahovlich to Montreal.

• • • Willie O'Ree: Cracking the Colour Barrier

Willie O'Ree became the first black athlete to play in the National Hockey League when he debuted with the Boston Bruins in 1958.

But breaking down the colour barrier in hockey, an accomplishment that often saw him referred to as "the Jackie Robinson of hockey," was not the New Brunswick native's only claim to fame.

Unknown to many, O'Ree played pro hockey for more than two decades without any vision in his right eye. Despite his disability, he was usually among the top scorers in the leagues he played in.

O'Ree was born in Fredericton on October 15, 1935, the youngest of thirteen children, and like many Canadians, he learned to play hockey on a backyard rink made with a garden hose by his father. He skated with the Fredericton Capitals Senior A team before playing junior hockey with the Quebec Frontenacs and Kitchener-Waterloo Canucks in the mid-1950s.

In 1956, after being scouted by Punch Imlach (later coach and general manager of the Toronto Maple Leafs), he turned professional with the Quebec Aces of the Quebec Hockey League and went on to a twenty-one-year pro career, which included parts of two seasons as a winger with the Boston Bruins.

When he played for the Bruins on January 18, 1958, wearing sweater No. 22, he became the first black man to play in the NHL before being shipped back to the Aces. He played in two games with the Bruins that season.

In 1956–57 O'Ree helped the Quebec Aces win the Duke of Edinburgh Trophy as QHL champs. In 1960–61, he was called up to the Bruins again, this time skating in forty-three games. In forty-five games with Boston he notched four goals and ten assists.

Much of his career was spent in

Courtesy of NHL Images

Willie O'Ree today. He lives in California.

the Western Hockey League, where he topped the thirty-goal mark four times.

Despite losing 97 percent of the sight in his eye after being hit by a puck while playing with the Kitchener-Waterloo Canucks, he won two WHL scoring titles — in 1964–65 when he notched thirty-eight goals and twenty-one assists for the Los Angeles Blades and in 1968–69 when he scored thirty-eight goals and forty-one assists for the San Diego Gulls. He was named to the WHL all-star team three times.

Remembering his days playing hockey in all-white leagues, O'Ree says, "I heard the racial remarks from players and fans. ... I wanted to concentrate on hockey and I soon found that the names never hurt unless you let them. I told myself 'I am proud of who I am and I can't change the colour of my skin.'"

O'Ree retired following the 1978–79 season, in which he played in fifty-three games with the San Diego Gulls of the Pacific Hockey League. Since then he has lived in the San Diego area, where he has dabbled in a handful of careers, including construction, athletic equipment sales, fast food outlet management, automobile sales, and security. A new career dawned in 1995, when he was hired as an ambassador for the NHL's diversity program.

O'Ree is director of Youth Development for NHL Diversity, a job that involves on- and off-ice clinics, speaking engagements, and personal appearances to introduce children with diverse ethnic backgrounds to hockey and help them pay for hockey equipment.

Since 1995, the program has involved more than forty thousand children in the U.S. and Canada, including goalie Gerald Coleman of Illinois, who played for

Courtesy of NHL Images

Willie O'Ree broke new ground when he suited up with the Boston Bruins in 1958.

the London Knights of the OHL and was drafted by the NHL's Tampa Bay Lightning in 2003.

O'Ree lives in La Mesa, California, a suburb of San Diego, with his wife, Deljeet, and daughter, Chandra. In 1999 he published a children's book, *The Autobiography of Willie O'Ree: Hockey's Black Pioneer*. A documentary, *Echoes in the Rink: The Willie O'Ree Story*, recounts his life.

In October 2005, he was among ten people named to the Order of New Brunswick.

WORTH NOTING...

Following his eye injury, doctors told O'Ree his career was finished. But he continued to play, and the only people who knew about his disability were his younger sister, Betty, of Montreal, and a close friend, Stan Maxwell, of Truro, Nova Scotia. His bad eye was replaced with a prosthesis in the early 1980s.

• • • Lui Passaglia: Hometown Boy Gets His Kicks

As a young boy, Vancouver native Lui Passaglia remembers hearing the sound of fans cheering on the B.C. Lions wafting over the walls of the old Empire Stadium. His father, who had emigrated from Italy, became a fan of the Lions and would occasionally sneak Passaglia in to watch games.

Fast forward to 1994, and the Grey Cup in another Vancouver stadium, BC Place, features the Lions and an all-American team, the Baltimore Stallions, battling it out. With the score tied at twenty-three and the last seconds of the game ticking off the clock, the hometown boy, Passaglia, steps on the field to try to win it with a thirty-eight-yard field goal. In the first Grey Cup to feature an American-based team, Canadian fans hold their collective breath as Passaglia makes contact.

Like he did so many times in his twenty-five-year career, the Vancouver kicker nailed it through the uprights, making the Lions CFL champions. In what was a long and fruitful career for the place-kicker/punter, Passaglia's 1994 last-second field goal is what most Canadians remember about him.

But as he says today from his office with the Lions club, where he works as director of community relations, you can't define a career by one kick. He acknowledges that the 1994 Grey Cup game was "a stand-out" and that it took on special meaning because it was Canada versus the U.S. "It was here in Vancouver, it was a pretty good spectacle, and we were the Cinderella team."

But Passaglia remembers other key moments in his career just as fondly: making the team for the first time in the mid-1970s after graduating from Simon Fraser

Passaglia doing what he did best.

University and being introduced as a player in his first game; his first Grey Cup played at BC Place in 1983; and the Lions winning in 1985 and the again in 2000 in Passaglia's last season.

When it was all over, Passaglia had set a CFL record (and, in fact, an all-pro football record) of 3,991 points, one that would stand up for some time. In his final year, as a forty-six-year-old, the kicker notched forty of forty-four field goals for an astounding 90.9 percent success rate.

As was the case with several CFL players in the 1980s, Passaglia received offers to go to the NFL. He declined, saying that the money wasn't much better south of the border in those days and that the Lions had made him a good offer. In 1988, he did try out for the Cleveland Browns and was also thinking of retiring, but the Lions still wanted him and offered a series of one-year contracts until he did retire.

Although he lasted longer than most kickers, by 2000 Passaglia says his body was telling him it was time to retire. He went to work for the Lions after retirement and found he missed playing the game for that first year. But now he enjoys being an armchair quarterback like other fans. In his post with the Lions, he still has a significant presence in Vancouver. Under his direction, the Lions are involved with literacy programs in elementary and high schools as well as connected with amateur football and charities throughout the province.

Courtesy of the BC Lions Football Club Inc.

Lui Passaglia grew up watching the B.C. Lions and later became the kicker who led the team to a Grey Cup victory.

It's a position he enjoys. "Even though I'm removed from the game I'm still involved with the players."

Passaglia, who was inducted into the CFL Hall of Fame in 2004, looks back fondly at his career. He admits he got butterflies before the games, but once he stepped on the field to make a crucial kick he stayed focused. "I was never nervous to go in and do my job. Once I was on the field, I thought I could make a difference."

And the Vancouver boy who dreamed of playing for the Lions and helping them win the Grey Cup certainly did.

"You couldn't ask for a better script," he says. "And to do it all in your hometown."

• • • Denis Potvin: Stellar NHL Blueliner

When the New York Islanders drafted Denis Potvin first overall in 1973, it was hoped the young defenceman from Ottawa would be a good foundation to improve the lowly expansion team that finished in last place in its first two years of play.

Potvin surpassed these expectations: during a fifteen-year career played entirely with the Islanders, he was one of the cornerstones that held the franchise together and eventually turned the team into a dynasty.

The former star of the Ottawa 67's of the Ontario Hockey Association (now the Ontario Hockey League) quickly became one of the most complete defenders to step onto the ice, helping the Islanders win four straight Stanley Cups from 1980 to 1983, along the way becoming the first NHL defenceman to score one thousand career points.

Potvin's wealth of natural talent allowed him to jump into the offensive rush while serving as a tough physical presence in his own end of the rink. His mean streak caused many an opposing forward to stay off his side of the ice.

At age fourteen, Potvin broke into the OHA with the 67's and played five seasons, beginning with the 1968–69 campaign. In his last season with Ottawa, he broke the scoring record for OHA defenceman with 123 points. He won two consecutive Kaminsky Awards as the league's premier rearguard.

Courtesy of FSN

Denis Potvin, right, is a colour analyst for Florida Panthers games on the Fox Sports Network with play-by-play announcer Dave Strader.

As an NHLer, he played in 1,060 regular season games, notching 310 goals and 742 assists, plus another 56 goals and 108 assists in the play-offs. In addition to four Stanley Cups, he won three Norris Trophies as the league's best defenceman, plus the Calder Trophy in 1974 as the league's best rookie.

In 1991 he was inducted into the Hockey Hall of Fame and Canada's Sports Hall of Fame. On March 31, 1988, a cheering crowd at the Nassau Coliseum on Long Island paid homage to his stellar career when his No. 5 sweater was hung from the rafters.

After retiring from the Islanders in 1988, he worked in New York City as a commercial real estate agent and stockbroker. He also worked part-time as an in-studio hockey analyst with the Sports Channel New York. In 1993, he became a colour analyst for the NHL's Florida Panthers and now works with the Fox Sports Network.

Potvin was living in the Fort Lauderdale, Florida, area with his wife, Valerie, daughters Madeleine and Annabelle, and son Christian. The family vacations from June to September at their summer home in Mont Tremblant, Quebec.

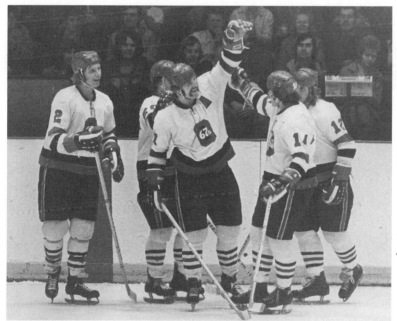

Courtesy of Denis Potvin

Denis Potvin, centre, early in his career as a star with the Ottawa 67's juniors.

• • • Manon Rheaume: Breaking the Ice

Manon Rheaume hasn't faced a blistering slapshot since 2000, but the woman who broke ground in North American sport by becoming the first female to play in a National Hockey League game is still close to the game she loves.

When the native of the Quebec City suburb of Lac Beauport inked a deal to play goal with the Tampa Bay Lightning in 1992, she became the first woman to sign a professional contract, the first to try out for an NHL team, and the first to play on a major men's professional team.

Rheaume, who was born on February 24, 1972, played in parts of two exhibition games with the Lightning — one period against the St. Louis Blues in 1992 and one period in 1993 against the Boston Bruins. In both games she allowed two goals.

She also helped backstop the Team Canada women's team to a silver medal at the 1998 Winter Olympics in Nagano, Japan, allowing four goals on fifty-four shots, and won gold medals at the World Championships in 1992 (1.72 goals-against average in four games) and 1994 (0.67 goals-against average in five games). She was named to the all-star team both years.

Courtesy of Hockey Hall of Fame

Manon Rheaume celebrates a win by Team Canada's women's team.

Rheaume began skating on her family's backyard rink at the age of four and by five was dressed up as a goaltender (snow pants, goalie gloves, and sometimes a helmet) so her two brothers could practise their slapshots. Her first stint as a goalie in organized hockey was in 1978 when she tended the nets for her brothers' team, coached by her father, Pierre.

She played with various boys' teams in the Quebec

City area, and in 1984, at age ten, practised with the Quebec Nordiques of the NHL and became the first girl to play in the Quebec International Pee Wee Hockey Tournament. She was regularly cut from top-level AA teams in favour of less talented boy goalies.

At nineteen, she became the first woman to play in a Junior A men's hockey game when she tended goal for the Trois-Rivières Draveurs of the Quebec Major Junior Hockey League, allowing three goals in the seventeen minutes she was between the pipes.

When she appeared in the Atlanta Knights' 4–1 loss to Salt Lake City in the International Hockey League on December 13, 1992, Rheaume became the first woman to play in a regular-season professional game.

Her pro career spanned 1992 to 1997 and saw her play twenty-four games for seven pro teams, the Atlanta Knights, Knoxville Cherokees, Nashville Knights, Las Vegas Aces, Tallahassee Tiger Sharks, Las Vegas Thunder, and Reno Renegades.

At five feet seven inches tall and 130 pounds — compared to male goalies who are often six feet tall and 200 pounds — Rheaume used quickness and a butterfly style to compensate for her smaller size.

Her pioneering efforts and good looks attracted worldwide attention. At one point she turned down an offer to pose for *Playboy* magazine.

After leaving hockey in 2000, Rheaume for three years was director of marketing in Irving, California, for Mission Hockey, where she helped market and develop hockey equipment for girls. She then worked for two years in Milwaukee as director of girls' hockey/marketing for POWERade Iceport, a sports complex that included rinks for hockey, figure skating, and roller hockey.

When the POWERade project stalled she looked for a new challenge and was hired in August 2005 as director of sales and marketing for the Central Collegiate Hockey Association in Farmington Hills, Michigan. Her job involves attracting corporate partners and demonstrating the potential of marketing their products and services in conjunction with the twelve-team college hockey association.

Rheaume is a single mother and lives with her six-year-old son, Dylan, in Northville, Michigan, about fifty kilometres from Detroit.

She knows she has helped the cause of women in the male-dominated world of sport but insists she is one of many females who have done their part, including golfers Annika Sorenstam and Michelle Wie and racing car driver Danica Patrick.

"I am one of a lot of women including the entire Canadian women's national [hockey] team who has helped the cause of women in professional sports ... but when I hear about young girls who say they have a poster of me in their bedroom and they want to be like me, it is most satisfying to think that I may make a difference in a girl's life."

WORTH NOTING...

In 2004, Rheaume coached a girls' all-star team that competed with boys' teams in an international Pee Wee tournament in Quebec. Her team reached the semifinals but was not invited back the following year.

Courtesy of Manon Rheaume

Rheaume lives in Michigan with her son, Dylan.

• • • Babe Ruth's First Home Run Baseball: The Sport's *Da Vinci Code*

Canada, and specifically Toronto, can lay claim to being the site of Babe Ruth's first professional home run. The Sultan of Swat hit his home run as a player with the Providence Grays at a baseball stadium at Hanlan's Point in Toronto on September 5, 1914.

The Babe's home run sailed over the fence, and most believe the ball landed in the waters of Lake Ontario. The Babe, of course, went on to fame as one of the greatest home run hitters in baseball history, but whatever happened to that first home run ball?

According to Scott Crawford, director of operations at Canada's Baseball Hall of Fame in St. Marys, Ontario, the ball sat in the water for at least seventy years. The story he's been told was that a diver fished the ball out of the lake sometime in the 1980s and brought it to the hall when it was then located in Toronto. Though no one could prove that the old ball brought in was in fact the same one the Babe hit, the hall displayed it as if it were authentic.

One day someone stole the ball from its display, and as he was being chased he tossed the ball back into Lake Ontario somewhere near Ontario Place. No one has attempted to dive for the ball since, says Crawford, and he doesn't know who found it in the first place.

Other sources claim that the ball on display wasn't the real deal anyway, and Crawford says that even if someone brought in a ball and claimed it was from Ruth's home run, it would probably be even harder today to prove it was authentic. Another theory is that ball was stolen, bronzed, and on display at a downtown Toronto bar, but again there seems to be no proof. There are others who believe the eyewitnesses to the home run who say it cleared the fence but didn't land in the water. Mike Filey, a well-known Toronto historian, says the fence was so close to the water a home run ball couldn't have gone anywhere else but into the lake.

In 2004, Toronto author Jerry Amernic's novel *The Gift of the Bambino* was published and dealt with the mystery of that home run ball. One critic referred to the mystery as baseball's *Da Vinci Code*.

Regardless of theories about the ball — it's near Hanlan's Point or

Ontario Place or even elsewhere — its likely home seems to be a watery grave.

AND ANOTHER THING...

The stadium at Hanlan's Point remained the home of the Maple Leafs, Toronto's minor league baseball team, until the mid-1920s when a new facility was built on the mainland. The grounds were used for picnics after that, and the stadium was torn down in 1937 to make way for the Toronto Island Airport. A plaque near the site commemorates the Ruth home run.

• • • Barbara Ann Scott:
Queen of the Ice Loves the Beach

Other than 2006, when speedskater Cindy Klassen won five medals at the Olympic Winter Games, 1948 may have seen the single greatest success for any Canadian athlete. That year, Barbara Ann Scott accomplished an unprecedented feat in figure skating history when she won the Canadian, North American, European, World, and Olympic titles.

Her talent on the ice and her winning smile endeared her to the hearts of Canadians, who more than fifty-five years later still haven't forgotten the former Ottawa champion. Scott, who married Tom King more than fifty years ago, still gets fan mail, and whenever she visits her home country she's inundated with requests for autographs, which she gladly signs. And several of those who contact her are girls born in the late 1940s and 1950s who were named Barbara after her.

Scott, who retired with her husband to Amelia Island, Florida, in the late 1990s, said in an interview from her home that she thinks she captured the imaginations and support of Canadians because she won so soon after the Second World War. Canada was looking for positive,

Courtesy of Library and Archives Canada, PA-112691

Few athletes in Canadian history were as popular or successful as figure skater Barbara Ann Scott.

upbeat news, and fans in her home country were behind her through-out all her victories, she says. "I felt like I wasn't skating for myself; it was for all these kind people who were wishing me well."

The Olympic gold medal at the St. Moritz Olympics was the real capper. She had to skate outdoors on a hockey rink, but her figures and jumps were clean and precise and better than anyone else's in the world.

When she came home, she was the toast of the country and a media star like none before her. Among the accolades she received was the design of a Barbara Ann Scott doll, many of which still exist and are collector's items. Scott still has a specially made one, as well as one in the form of a bear that has the name "Bearbara" on its figure skates. She laughs at the tribute, noting that "the feet [on that doll] are enormous."

After her amateur triumphs, she skated professionally for another seven years before hanging up the blades. In her post-Olympics world, she lived in Chicago, where Tom developed a successful commercial real estate business. Barbara Ann was a professional figure skating judge for a while with fellow Olympic champion Dick Button, but she also made her name in the world of horse shows, where she won hundreds of ribbons and trophies.

Despite these accomplishments, she's hesitant to speak of her suc-cesses, letting husband Tom do the talking about that. "She was an extraordinary rider," he says. Tom says his wife has virtually no ego, but that whenever they visit Canada "they call me Mr. Scott and I love it."

The two decided to settle in Amelia Island, near Jacksonville, after visiting it several years ago and "absolutely falling in love with the area," she says. With a condo right on the ocean, Scott enjoys the beach and games of golf. The couple are also regular visitors to the Jacksonville symphony as well as the island's two theatres.

The famed Canadian athlete still watches figure skating occasionally and says there have been many champions since her time that she admired, mentioning Peggy Fleming and Michelle Kwan as two of them. In 2004, Barbara Ann and Tom established a scholarship at her former club, the Minto Skating Club in Ottawa. In 2006, she was a guest of the Canadian championships in Ottawa as well as an honorary chair of the Worlds competition in Calgary. She enjoys visiting with skaters during these sojourns to Canada and mentions how former champion Kurt

Browning calls the couple "grams and gramps." "I'm grandmother to all our champions," she says.

A member of Canada's Sports Hall of Fame and an Officer of the Order of Canada, Barbara Ann Scott has a legacy in this country that seemingly won't be forgotten. These days, "life is wonderful," she says, as she gazes out at the ocean and beach that are home. For the future she hopes to "live happily on Amelia Island and enjoy what's left of our lives."

• • • Linda Thom: Straightshooter

Linda Thom became a household name in Canada when she won a gold medal in sport pistol shooting at the 1984 Olympic Games in Los Angeles.

It was the first Summer Olympics gold medal won by Canada since 1968, the first gold won by an individual Canadian athlete since 1956, and the first won by a Canadian woman in the Summer Games since 1928.

Following the Olympics, Thom was awarded the Velma Springstead Trophy as Canada's 1984 female athlete of the year. Prior to those games she won a string of other honours, including four gold, two silver, and two bronze medals in World Cup events and a silver and a bronze at the 1983 Pan American Games. She broke the world record in the Federation of the Americas championships in 1973 and won another gold medal in 1985.

Over the years the native of Hamilton, Ontario, who now lives in Ottawa, has demonstrated that accuracy with a pistol and rifle is just one of her many talents.

In 1975, she graduated from the Cordon Bleu School of Cooking in Paris and for nine years ran a cooking school and catering business in Ottawa; she founded the Society of American Wines in 1980; and in

Photo by Randy Ray

Linda Thom, now a skilled chef and real estate agent, lives near an Ottawa park that bears her name and displays an oversized replica of the Olympic gold medal she won in 1984.

1995 she ran for provincial office as a member of the Conservative party, losing to Liberal Dalton McGuinty, who later became Ontario's premier. Thom was awarded the Order of Canada in 1985.

She lives several kilometres south of Parliament Hill with her husband, Donald, opposite a park that bears her name. For the past seventeen years she has sold real estate for Royal LePage.

She no longer shoots but occasionally coaches others aspiring to "go for the gold." She also instructs downhill skiers at Camp Fortune, north of Ottawa in Quebec's Gatineau Hills, and was on the board of directors of a local epicurean group that hands out awards to local restaurants and bistros.

Thom, who has worn glasses since she was six years old, says she knows why she was a successful athlete and loves to pass along the keys to success. She gives credit to unfailing support at home, starting with her husband. "You'll never forgive yourself for not trying," he urged when it was decided that women's shooting events would be added to the Olympics for the first time in 1984. Participating in the Games meant coming out of retirement after seven years away from the sport. Other factors were financial support from Sport Canada, excellent coaching, a positive mentality, and the ability to focus and "really believe I could win."

• • • Whit Tucker:
One of Russ Jackson's Favourite Targets

Whit Tucker has gone from flanker to personal financial advisor.

Once a speedy wide receiver who teamed with Ottawa Rough Rider quarterbacks such as Russ Jackson to march the ball into the end zone, Tucker is a senior vice-president and investment advisor with BMO Nesbitt Burns in Ottawa.

A graduate of the University of Western Ontario in London, Ontario, Tucker was twenty-one years old when he joined the Rough Riders in 1962 as a defensive back before donning sweater No. 26 and becoming a popular pass catcher with the Canadian Football League team.

By the time the Windsor, Ontario, native retired in 1970, he'd caught 272 passes for 6,092 yards and scored 53 touchdowns as a receiver in 121 regular season games. Football greats he played with included speedy running back Ron Stewart and Jackson.

Courtesy of Canadian Football League Hall of Fame and Museum

Whit Tucker was a sure-handed receiver for the Ottawa Rough Riders. He now works in the finance industry.

For eight seasons, Tucker was one of Jackson's favourite downfield targets. Jackson's accuracy and Tucker's reliable hands helped the latter score a touchdown on every third catch he made. When he left the game he was averaging 22.4 yards per reception, still a CFL record among players who have caught at least two hundred passes.

Statistically, his best season was in 1967, when he hauled in 52 passes for 1,171 yards and 9 touchdowns. His best year for regular season scoring was 1968, when he took the ball into the end zone thirteen times. His longest reception came that same year when he caught a pass that moved the ball ninety-four yards up the field. He helped Ottawa win the Grey Cup in 1968 and 1969, when Frank Clair coached the team.

Tucker has been in the financial planning business since 1964 and for more than thirty years was a branch manager with Burns Brothers and Denton, which became Burns Fry Ltd. in 1976 and BMO Nesbitt Burns in 1994.

He has served on the board of the Ottawa Airport Authority and the YM-YWCA in Ottawa, and has been a member of the board of directors of the Ottawa Civic Hospital, including two years as its chairman. Now in his mid-sixties, he has a son and three daughters and six grandchildren.

He was once a season ticket holder with the Ottawa Renegades, which folded in 2006. These days he prefers to spend time at his cottage in the 1000 Islands in eastern Ontario.

PLACES
• • •
Revisiting Old Hangouts

• • • First Flagship Canadian Tire Store: More Than Just Tires

We take Canadian Tire for granted these days. With some 460 retail stores across Canada and a national presence as one of the country's leading retailers, Canadian Tire is part of our culture. Who hasn't gone off to one of these stores to buy auto parts, barbecue tools, or sports equipment? Who hasn't stashed Canadian Tire money in a car's glove compartment or made fun of the know-it-all actor featured in the company's television commercials until early 2006?

But the road to becoming a national icon is long. Back in 1922, brothers John W. and Alfred J. Billes bought out Hamilton Tire and

Canadian Tire's original flagship store in Toronto, pictured here, was replaced in 2003 by a larger and more modern outlet.

Garage Ltd. at the corner of Gerrard and Hamilton streets in Toronto, the first step in establishing the Canadian Tire company. The shop sold repair parts, tires, batteries, and homemade antifreeze at a time when there were about forty thousand cars in the city.

The brothers then moved operations to Bloor Street West, then to Yonge Street, installing a gas pump at the first of two Yonge and Isabella locations. In 1927, they incorporated the company as Canadian Tire, a name they chose "because it sounded big," according to the company's history. As other Canadians became interested in ordering from the store, Canadian Tire launched its first catalogue in 1928. The catalogue is still a common browsing material in millions of Canadian households today.

Although the company set up an associate store in Hamilton, Ontario, in 1924, it was three years later that it reached a notable milestone by establishing its first flagship store at 837 Yonge Street in Toronto. Canadian Tire gained a reputation as the store where clerks wore roller skates, a technique used to speed up service from the large stock floor to the sales counter.

From then on the company rarely looked back, eventually spreading across Canada. As for that first flagship store, it was renovated and transformed in 2002 into a new, larger Canadian Tire on the same site. The new flagship store was officially opened April 24, 2003, with 65,000 square feet of retail space.

For more information on Canadian Tire visit www.canadiantire.ca.

Photo by Mark Kearney

Canadian Tire is an icon in this country's business world.

• • • Canada's Hockey Shrines: Revered Arenas

They are places of memory: the hallowed buildings where dreams came true for thousands of kids who wanted to be the ones who shot and scored their way into Canadians' collective consciousness. It is in these arenas that hockey grew to be a truly national sport and where fans gathered by the thousands to root for the home teams and often boo the visitors.

NHL squads no longer skate in any of the following shrines to our national sport, but these snapshots of edifices from another era can help us remember their glory days.

The Stampede Corral
Built: 1949–50
Cost: $1.5 million
Last NHL home team: Calgary Flames
Location: Calgary Stampede and Exhibition Grounds in Calgary, Alberta
Capacity for hockey: 7,242

The Corral was built as the home of the Calgary Stampeders hockey club to replace the outdated but well used Victoria Arena, which also served as a horse show and livestock building. For a time it was the largest arena west of Toronto.

It was designed with seating for 6,650 and room for 2,200 standing. All of the seats, which were arranged in colour-coded sections to indicate the price range of the tickets, had an unobstructed view of the ice surface.

The arena was officially opened December 26, 1950, with a Western Hockey League contest between the Calgary Stampeders and Edmonton Flyers.

When the NHL's Atlanta Flames moved to Calgary in 1980, the Corral was renovated and became the home ice for the Calgary Flames until 1983, when the team moved to the Saddledome, now known as the Pengrowth Saddledome.

The building, which is located a short walk from the Saddledome, is no longer the home base for a hockey team. It hosts a variety of sporting and entertainment events and as a concert venue it seats 6,500 people.

Edmonton Gardens
Built: 1913
Cost: $1.5 million
Last WHA home team: Alberta/Edmonton Oilers
Location: Northlands Park in Edmonton, Alberta
Capacity for hockey: 5,200

Edmonton Gardens was home to the upstart World Hockey Association's Alberta Oilers (later the Edmonton Oilers) from 1972 to 1974, when the team moved to the Northlands Coliseum, now Rexall Place.

When the building opened in 1913, it was called the Livestock Pavilion, with seating for three thousand people. Locals boasted that it had the biggest ice surface in Canada. Affectionately known as "the arena" by visitors, it was home ice for the Dominion Furriers and the Edmonton Eskimos hockey teams.

The building underwent major renovations after the Second World War. Following a hockey revival that began when the Edmonton Flyers franchise became active, additions were made, and along with a new face, the building got a new name: Edmonton Gardens. It remained untouched until it was demolished in the early 1980s to make way for Northlands Agricom, which is still in operation today at Northlands Park.

Over the years the building also housed the Edmonton Oil Kings junior hockey team. But its most high profile tenant was the Alberta Oilers, which became the Edmonton Oilers in 1973 and joined the NHL in 1979 when the WHA folded.

Montreal Forum
Built: 1924
Cost: $1.5 million
Last NHL home team: Montreal Canadiens

Location: 2313 Saint Catherine Street West in Montreal, Quebec
Capacity for hockey: 17,959

The Montreal Forum was the home of the NHL's Montreal Canadiens from 1926 to 1996 and housed the NHL's Montreal Maroons from 1924 to 1938. The Canadiens won twenty-two of their twenty-four Stanley Cups while the Forum was their home rink. The Maroons won two cups during their stay at the Forum.

The building, which has been called "Montreal's holiest shrine," also had a reputation as one of the most renowned performance venues in North America. It was built on the site of a former open-air roller skating palace.

The Canadiens played the first game hosted at the Forum on November 29, 1924, and became full-time tenants two years later. The building originally sat 9,300 spectators, and over the years its capacity was boosted to more than 18,000, including standing room, although at one game the crowd numbered more than 19,000.

When the Canadiens moved to the Molson Centre (now the Bell Centre) in March 1996, the building was completely gutted inside and converted into a downtown entertainment centre, the Pepsi Forum. Centre ice has been recreated in the centre of the complex, while the Forum's original stands are scattered throughout. It is home to the Quebec Walk of Fame, honouring such celebrities as Celine Dion and Maurice Richard, and its Atwater Street entrance has a large bronze Montreal Canadiens logo surrounded by twenty-four bronze Stanley Cup banners cemented into the sidewalk. Inscribed in French are the words "Forever proud."

The entire building is designed to honour the Forum's storied history, with special emphasis on the Canadiens. The largest tenants are a movie theatre with twenty-two screens, an electronics and appliance outlet, and a liquor store.

In early 2006, with more than one-third of its commercial space vacant, the building was sold for $45 million to a New York–based investment group.

Ottawa Civic Centre
Built: 1967–68
Cost: $8.9 million
Last NHL home team: Ottawa Senators
Location: 1015 Bank Street, Lansdowne Park, in Ottawa, Ontario
Capacity for hockey: 9,862

Located within the Lansdowne Park complex next to the Rideau Canal, the Civic Centre has been the home of the Major Junior A Ottawa 67's of the Ontario Hockey League since the team's inception in 1967.

Following a series of renovations the building was home base for the modern-day version of the NHL's Ottawa Senators from 1992 until 1995, when the team moved to the Palladium, a new building in the west Ottawa suburb of Kanata, later renamed the Corel Centre and now known as Scotiabank Place.

The Civic Centre also housed the WHA's Ottawa Nationals for the 1972–73 season, and in 1976 the rink was briefly the home of another WHA team, the Ottawa Civics, which folded about two weeks after being moved to Ottawa from Denver.

With total attendance surpassing 2 million, the facility hosts hundreds of events annually, including 67's games, trade shows, and concerts.

Quebec Colisée
Built: 1949
Cost: unknown
Last NHL home team: Quebec Nordiques
Location: 250 boulevard Wilfrid-Hamel in Quebec City
Capacity for hockey: 15,570

The Quebec Colisée was the home of the Quebec Nordiques from 1972 to 1995 and currently houses the Quebec Remparts of the Quebec Major Junior Hockey League. The Nordiques left the building in 1995 when the team was moved to Denver, Colorado.

The original Colisée was erected early in the twentieth century. In

1949 it burned down and was replaced on the same site by a ten-thousand-seat arena. The first Colisée housed several teams, including the Quebec Bulldogs of the National Hockey Association, winners of two Stanley Cups, and the Quebec Aces, which played in the Quebec Senior Hockey League before joining the AHL in 1959.

The Colisée was heavily renovated in 1980, raising capacity to 15,750 to meet NHL standards when the Nordiques moved from the WHA to the NHL.

The building was renamed Colisée Pepsi in November of 1999 and now hosts a variety of cultural activities, including concerts and trade shows.

Maple Leaf Gardens
Built: 1931–32
Cost: $1.5 million
Last NHL home team: Toronto Maple Leafs
Location: Carlton and Church streets in Toronto, Ontario
Capacity for hockey: 16,000

Maple Leaf Gardens has been mostly dormant since February 13, 1999, when the Toronto Maple Leafs played their final game at the historic

Maple Leaf Gardens, long-time home of the Toronto Maple Leafs.

rink and moved to the Air Canada Centre, although it has hosted some ice hockey and lacrosse matches.

It was home to the Leafs for sixty-seven years and also housed the Toronto Toros of the WHA from 1974 to 1976, the Toronto Marlboroughs of the OHL, and the Toronto Huskies in their single season in the National Basketball Association. The NBA's Toronto Raptors played a handful of games at the Gardens between 1995 and 1999.

Since the Leafs' departure, various redevelopment schemes have been proposed, including condominium towers rising through the roof, a building supplies store, and an entertainment complex containing retail shops and cinemas. All were abandoned when it was discovered that removal of the interior seating would weaken the building's walls.

One of two "original six" hockey rinks in Canada, "the Carlton Street Cashbox," as it was nicknamed, is owned by Loblaw Companies, which plans to build a supermarket in the space where packed houses of 16,000-plus fans cheered for the Leafs for more than six decades. Plans are expected to be unveiled in 2006 that will preserve the exterior, including its marquee and the Maple Leafs logos on the roof. The project is expected to include a three-level supermarket and two levels of parking, a fitness centre, a liquor store, and a post office.

Pacific Coliseum
Built: 1966–67
Cost: $6 million
Last NHL home team: Vancouver Canucks
Location: 100 North Renfrew Street in Vancouver, B.C.
Capacity for hockey: 16,150

The Pacific Coliseum, located on the Pacific National Exhibition grounds, was the home of the Vancouver Canucks of the NHL from 1972 to 1994. The rink also housed the Vancouver Blazers of the WHA from 1973 to 1975.

Instead of being rectangular in shape like many rinks of the era, the Coliseum was circular, providing a good view of the ice from every seat in the building.

The Pacific Coliseum, former home of the Vancouver Canucks.

Since the Canucks moved to General Motors Place in 1995, the Coliseum has continued to host a variety of events, including concerts by stars like Bruce Springsteen, Green Day, Shania Twain, and the Doors. It is also the home of the Vancouver Giants of the Western Hockey League's Junior A loop.

The building has been chosen as the venue for figure skating in the 2010 Winter Olympics, which will take place in Vancouver and neighbouring communities.

Winnipeg Arena
Built: 1955
Cost: unknown
Last NHL home team: Winnipeg Jets
Location: 1430 Maroons Road in Winnipeg, Manitoba
Capacity for hockey: 15,565

Winnipeg Arena was the home of the Winnipeg Jets of the WHA and the NHL from 1972 to 1996. Following the departure of the Jets to Phoenix, Arizona, the arena's prime tenant was the Manitoba Moose of the International Hockey League, now the American Hockey League.

The Winnipeg Arena was also home to the Winnipeg Warriors of the WHL from 1980 through 1984. A popular location for filming movies, the building was used for the made-for-TV movie *Inside the Osmonds* and the ESPN film *A Season on the Brink*.

The original arena seated 10,100 patrons. Renovations in 1979 expanded capacity to 15,565. After the Jets left in 1996, another renovation added pricey club seats, and the north end ice level seats were replaced with a club lounge. Capacity was actually decreased to 9,777, as the upper decks were no longer used.

Winnipeg Arena earned the nickname of the "White House" among locals for its traditional "White Out" during Jets' playoff games, when fans would wear white clothing in support of the home team.

With the opening of the new MTS Centre, the Winnipeg Arena became redundant. It hosted its last event on November 7, 2004; demolition was completed in early 2006. The Ontario Teachers' Pension Plan Board purchased the site for $3.6 million.

• • • Tim Hortons: The Dawn of Donuts

Tim Horton, a star defenceman with several NHL teams, including the Toronto Maple Leafs and the Buffalo Sabres, opened his first donut outlet at 65 Ottawa Street North in Hamilton, Ontario.

In the early days it was a tiny, rather nondescript building with three awnings and a small parking lot. Over the years it has been renovated several times to allow new equipment and products to be added and to maintain safety standards. It is operational today and looks like any other of the donut chain's outlets, with brown brick and the distinctive red Tim Hortons signature across the front.

Horton, who died in a car crash in 1974, launched his donut business in February 1964, and two months later he and two partners opened the first Tim Hortons franchise outlet, where a dozen donuts cost sixty-nine cents and a cup of coffee was a dime. Ex-policeman Ron Joyce, who eventually took over the chain, was the first successful franchisee of Tim Hortons, Store No. 1.

At an October 1999 ceremony to reopen the store after its latest round of renovations, Ottawa Street North was given the honorary name Tim Hortons Way. Special signage, including a plaque on the front of the building, was unveiled to signify the heritage of the store; permanent display cases featuring Tim Hortons memorabilia can be seen inside.

Courtesy of TDL Group Corp.

Canada's first Tim Hortons outlet in Hamilton, Ontario, in its early days. It has been renovated serveral times since this picture was taken and is still going strong.

WORTH NOTING...

From humble beginnings, Tim Hortons has grown into a major chain with more than 2,500 locations in Canada and nearly 300 in the U.S. states of Connecticut, New York, Kentucky, Ohio, Maine, Pennsylvania, Massachusetts, West Virginia, Michigan, and Rhode Island.

• • • Canada's First McDonald's Restaurant: Still Flipping Burgers

The Golden Arches made their debut in Canada on June 1, 1967, when the first McDonald's restaurant opened on No. 3 Road in Richmond, B.C.

McDonald's entry into the Canadian market came nineteen years after brothers Richard and Maurice McDonald opened their first drive-in hamburger joint in San Bernardino, California, and twelve years after the late Ray Kroc, founder of the chain as we know it today, opened his first outlet in Des Plaines, Illinois.

The Richmond, B.C., location was originally a takeout restaurant with three serving windows where a hamburger could be picked up for eighteen cents. Its exterior was clad in red and white tiles.

George Tidball, licensee for the outlet, had a minor panic attack before the outlet swung open its doors for the first time. "I thought, 'What have I done? What if nobody shows up,'" he said in a 1992 article in McDonald's *Celebrating 25 Years in Canada* magazine.

The first week saw so many customers flock to the restaurant that Tidball ran out of meat by the first weekend. He had to close down and give rain checks for free hamburgers to disappointed customers.

In 1975, the Richmond outlet was rebuilt on the same spot with brick walls and a cottage-style roof and had room for three hundred hungry

Courtesy of McDonald's® Restaurants of Canada Limited

The first McDonald's restaurant in Canada in Richmond, British Columbia, as it appeared in its early years.

diners. Its Playland was upgraded in 1984, and by 1987 the restaurant was designed in contemporary style and had a unique conveyor belt drive-thru that transported hamburgers, french fries, and beverages to an area of the parking lot where customers were hungrily awaiting their food.

Several other renovations have taken place in the past twenty years, and the outlet is still going strong.

In 2006, McDonald's had nearly 1,400 restaurants in Canada that employed more than 77,000 people.

WORTH NOTING...

George Tidball, who ran Canada's first McDonald's outlet, went on to found the Keg 'n Cleaver chain of California-style steak and lobster houses, which opened its first location in North Vancouver, B.C., on June 21, 1971. The business later changed its name to the Keg Steakhouse & Bar.

AND ANOTHER THING...

The first McDonald's opened by Ray Kroc in Des Plaines, Illinois, in 1955 no longer serves hamburgers and fries. The building is a museum containing McDonald's memorabilia and artifacts, including the milk-shake mixers Kroc sold before he took the concept of fast food to the masses.

MUSIC
• • •
Off the Charts

• • • Chad Allan: Shakin' All Over — With Seniors

In the 1960s, he rocked the house as lead singer of Chad Allan and the Expressions, the Guess Who, and Brave Belt, backed by a drummer and a couple of wailing electric guitars. One of the most memorable songs he belted out was "Shakin' All Over," which has sold more than 2 million copies.

Today, Allan is more apt to be playing an accordion or piano and crooning tunes like "It's a Long Way to Tipperary" and "Bye Bye Blackbird" for seniors, though his repertoire does include the occasional up-tempo tune.

Allan's venues are senior citizens' homes, adult day care centres, and hospitals, where he performs an average of four times a week, which is fine with the Canadian rock 'n' roll legend, who, in his early sixties and with snow white hair, is an early senior.

"When I was younger doing the seniors thing wasn't all that desirable," he says. "But I soon discovered it can be spiritually rewarding. As a young senior, I can understand and appreciate the needs and wants of older people."

Allan began playing seniors' facilities fifteen years ago. It's now his main source of income. At most seniors' gigs, he starts on the accordion he has owned since he was a kid and eventually switches to piano, doing songs such as "Last Date," Floyd Cramer's instrumental hit from the 1960s. Sometimes he does an instrumental rendition of Henry

Mancini's "Moon River," before going back to his musical roots with rollicking versions of Big Joe Turner's "Flip, Flop and Fly," Ray Charles's "What'd I Say," and Jerry Lee Lewis's "Great Balls of Fire."

Canadian music fans will remember Allan as front man for the Expressions and later the Guess Who and Brave Belt, which became Bachman-Turner Overdrive, before either had any sustained success. He quit both bands and pretty much left the touring and performing side of business after he blew his voice in the Guess Who by screaming loud rock 'n' roll for years on end. He can still sing today but admits his voice sounds a little rough.

"It's a miracle that I can even speak, never mind sing," says Allan, who grew up in Winnipeg and has lived in the Vancouver area since 1977.

After losing most of his voice Allan admits to becoming "a bit of a hermit" who lived with his parents and performed mainly at restaurants. Along the way, he earned a bachelor of science degree at the University of Manitoba and an honours degree in psychology from the University of Winnipeg.

Courtesy of Chad Allan

The isolated stage of his life ended when he met and married his wife, Christine, in 1999. He taught songwriting in several locations, including Kwantlen University College in Richmond and Douglas College in New Westminster, but now only does seniors' shows.

Allan's musical career started with a number of successful bands in Winnipeg but really began to click when guitarist Randy Bachman joined his rock and roll group the Silvertones. Allan and the Silvertones evolved into Chad Allan and the Reflections and then Chad Allan and the Expressions.

Guess who's playing accordion at seniors' homes gigs these days? Chad Allan, formerly of the most famous band to come out of Winnipeg.

The Expressions scored a North American hit with "Shakin' All Over" in 1965, but no one knew them as Chad Allan and the Expressions, so radio station copies of the record showed the words "Guess Who?" with no band name. Listeners were invited to guess who the band was; eventually their name evolved to the Guess Who, and the name stuck.

Allan quit the Guess Who in 1966 because of voice problems and his distaste for travelling. He became a backup singer on CBC-TV show *Music Hop*, and when the show changed its name to *Let's Go* he became the host and sang hits of the day with the Guess Who as his backing band. After Randy Bachman left the Guess Who in 1970, Allan and Bachman formed Brave Belt, which recorded two albums before Allan left the band.

Allan and his wife live in an apartment in Burnaby, B.C., just outside of Vancouver. He is writing and stockpiling songs that he hopes to sell to other artists or to perform himself.

IN CASE YOU WERE WONDERING...

Chad Allan was born Allan Kowbel. Tired of his friends calling him "cow bell," he adapted the stage name Chad Allan after 1950s and 1960s American folk singer Chad Mitchell.

• • • Bernie Barbe: Cops and Rockers

Bernie Barbe busted nearly one hundred people during his twelve-year career with the Royal Canadian Mounted Police, but slapping handcuffs on Rolling Stones guitarist Keith Richards in 1977 was by far his most memorable arrest.

Now an international security expert, Barbe was a young constable with the RCMP's drug squad assigned to Toronto airport when he became involved in one of the most famous celebrity busts on Canadian soil.

Events began to unfold on February 24, 1977, when Richards's common-law wife, Anita Pallenberg, was nabbed at the airport with marijuana and heroin in her luggage. She was on her way to join Richards, who was in Toronto with the Stones to record some tracks at the El Mocambo club for a live album.

Three days later, Barbe and fellow plainclothes constables Pete Hadley and Bill Seward were sent to the Harbour Castle Hotel on Toronto's waterfront with a search warrant for Richards's suite. After

Courtesy of Bernie Barbe

being admitted by Pallenberg, Barbe strolled into the bedroom where the Rolling Stone was sleeping and saw fresh drug residue, drug wrappings, and drug paraphernalia in a garbage bin.

When he shook the guitarist by the shoulder to wake him up, Richards lunged at Hadley, at which point Barbe gently nudged him back onto the bed.

"It was a perfectly normal reaction. You are in a deep sleep, you suddenly see a stranger by your bed and you react. It was not a big issue," recalls Barbe, who was the arresting officer that

Bernie Barbe arrested Rolling Stone Keith Richards in 1977. The former RCMP officer lives in Ottawa.

day and for most of his career was involved mainly in routine arrests of illegal immigrants and drug users far less famous than Richards.

The rock star was told to dress himself and was informed that he was under arrest. He was handcuffed and taken to the RCMP office at the airport, where he was charged with possession of drugs with intent to traffic.

"On the way, we discussed music and his guitars … he was a real gentleman," says Barbe, who found twenty-two grams of heroin and five grams of cocaine in Richards's hotel room.

Richards was released on bail and appeared in a Toronto courtroom in October 1978 where he pleaded guilty to drug possession. His sentence could have been seven years to life in jail, but in return for a guilty plea, the judge ordered Richards to perform for free to benefit the Canadian National Institute for the Blind and enroll in a drug rehabilitation program.

In the House of Commons, former prime minister John Diefenbaker called the sentence "preposterous."

Richards fulfilled his obligations and later said publicly that his arrest on that cold and rainy Toronto morning in 1977 was a turning point that helped him beat his addiction.

In the years that followed, Richards continued to rock with the Stones, and Barbe held various positions with the RCMP in Toronto and Montreal before joining the Canadian Security and Intelligence Service in Ottawa (CSIS) in 1985, where his work included internal security investigations and monitoring the activities of the KGB. From 1990 to 1993 he was a CSIS liaison officer based in Bonn, Germany, and from 1993 until his retirement in 2001 he worked in various sections of CSIS in Ottawa.

Since 2001 Barbe, who is in his mid-fifties, has owned and operated Rempart Security Consulting in Ottawa. He is an expert on airport and port security and has worked in Africa, Thailand, Brussels, and other countries, where he has helped develop and implement security strategies and taught security courses.

In August of 2005, Barbe took his wife, Sue Browne, to a Rolling Stones concert at Lansdowne Park in Ottawa to celebrate her birthday. It was the first time he'd seen Richards in person since the historic 1977 bust.

"You look at the guy up there on stage … you think of how all through his career he impacted a whole generation of people. To say for a little blip on the history charts I had up-close dealings is really quite something."

WORTH NOTING...

Prior to busting Keith Richards, Barbe was involved in another fairly high profile takedown. In the summer of 1976, he arrested Don Murdoch of the New York Rangers at Toronto airport after a customs officer found a small quantity of cocaine in a pair of folded-up socks in the hockey player's suitcase.

• • • The Bells: They've Stayed Awhile

The country-flavoured tune that got turned into a smoky guy/girl ballad got recorded only because Cliff Edwards of the Bells begged for studio time, and it wasn't intended to be a single until a radio station executive who was the then-queen of the airwaves suggested it should be.

Some thirty-five years after "Stay Awhile" rocketed up the charts to number one in Canada and number seven on the Billboard charts, Edwards recalls with fondness the strange journey the tune took to make his group, the Bells, a household name in North America. The Montreal-based group had already scored a minor hit with "Moody Manitoba Morning" and bigger success with "Fly Little White Dove, Fly."

The latter song and "Stay Awhile" got recorded only because Edwards was able to convince Polydor Records to give them some extra studio time. An executive who was leaving the company anyway granted Edwards's wish figuring he had nothing to lose. "I had an idea that a guy-girl approach to ["Stay Awhile"] was really going to be our ticket," Edwards said in an interview of how the song was recorded.

While "Fly Little White Dove, Fly" was gaining popularity in Canada, the Bells were performing one night in Windsor, Ontario. The sparse audience included Rosalie Tremblay of influential radio station CKLW. She told the band that "Stay Awhile" should be the next single, and given that she was arguably the most influential person in radio in North America, the Bells listened. "If she said 'Stay Awhile' was what she wanted we told the record company that's what they should do," Edwards recalled. "It was a huge hit."

The Bells were on their way, making appearances on the *Tonight Show* and the *Merv Griffin Show* among others. While they released a few other singles, nothing matched the success they'd already tasted. Edwards left the group in 1973 for a solo career that included a couple of albums, while Jacki Ralph (Edwards's sister-in-law and the "girl" voice in "Stay Awhile") kept versions of the group going until 1981.

But that wasn't the last fans heard of the Bells. The group reunited for a couple of concerts in the late 1980s and have gotten together for a several performances in the past few years. A *Best of the Bells* CD came out a couple of years ago.

The concerts these days are "more of a theatrical production," Edwards explained, in which he comes on stage to reminisce about singing in Montreal in the 1960s before being joined by band members to play the hits. "I love it," he said of performing now. "I'm pretty pleased with the way we sound."

Other than performing, Edwards has dabbled in several careers. He worked as a cameraman for CTV based out of Kingston, Ontario, and managed a theatre in Wingham, Ontario, for several years before moving back to Kingston to manage the Grand Theatre there. He also worked as a tourism director for Kingston, and in early 2006 he bought a 225-seat restaurant, MacNeil's Landing, which he says has been an exciting enterprise so far. He has two homes in and around the Kingston area.

His ex-wife, Anne, who was also in the Bells, lives in Kingston working in pastoral care at the Hotel Dieux Hospital. Jacki Ralph lives in Vancouver where she runs an animal hospital with her husband. Doug Gravelle, the Bells' drummer, lives in Ganonoque, Ontario, where he is a partner/owner of a flooring business. Frank Mills, who performed with the Bells for a while and had a huge solo career as an instrumental recording star with such hits as "Music Box Dancer," is believed to be living in the Bahamas.

AND ANOTHER THING...

Though mild by today's standards, "Stay Awhile" was banned on some radio stations in the early 1970s because programmers thought it was too risqué. The idea of a man and woman being in the same room at night and her dropping "her robe on the floor" was apparently too sensual for their listeners.

• • • First CHUM Chart: A Hit with Listeners

Rock music fans growing up in and around Toronto from the late 1950s to the early 1980s more than likely considered the weekly CHUM Chart their music bible.

Each week music buffs would pore over a listing of the top songs, which showed their position relative to the previous week and how long they'd been on the chart. In 1957, Toronto's CHUM became the first twenty-four-hour-a-day hit parade station in Canada, and on May 27 of that year issued its first CHUM Chart. The simple folded "pocket charts" listed the top fifty songs of the week but by 1968 had reduced that to the top thirty. In 1975, the pocket charts were ended and listings appeared in newspapers.

The first chart had a "white background, with black and orange high-lighted areas," says Brad Jones, program director at 1050 CHUM. "The 'disc jockey cat' Clementine appears on the very first chart and every weekly chart for the next three years or so. The concept of the weekly hit parade was just an extension of the on-air presentation of the songs."

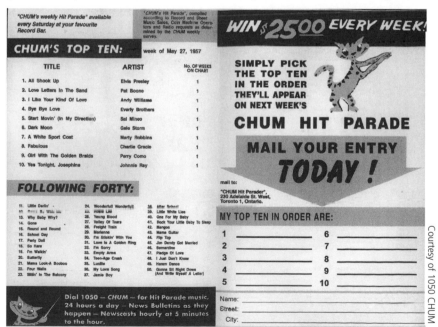

This replica of the first CHUM Chart shows that Elvis Presley was king of the singles back in 1957.

Topping the chart on May 27, 1957, was "All Shook Up" by Elvis Presley, and according to *The CHUM Chart Book* by Ron Hall, Presley would go on to have eighty-five charted songs by the time the station ended its listings in 1983. The last chart topper in December 1983 was "Say Say Say" by Paul McCartney, who coincidentally had the second most charted songs ever on CHUM (including his records with the Beatles and Wings), with seventy-six hits.

The station, which is playing oldies to this day, has that original CHUM Chart in its archives along with a full set of every one since. "As for how many of the original charts are out there is anybody's guess and for a value, no idea," says Jones. "An item is only worth something when someone is willing to pay for it."

WORTH NOTING...

Paul Anka, with his hit song "Diana," was the first Canadian musician to top the CHUM Chart back in August 12, 1957. He was also the top Canadian in terms of songs charted, with thirty-eight. The next best Canadians were the Guess Who, with twenty-two charted songs.

• • • Clubs Worth Remembering: Fading to Silence

Every generation has its favourite clubs and bars for hanging out, drinking, and listening to great tunes from musicians on their way up or who have attained some level of stardom. For those of us lucky enough to have heard great music from the 1960s and 1970s in the following venues, the memories linger even if the clubs do not.

The Cave

A Vancouver fixture in the 1950s, 1960s, and 1970s, the Cave featured a wealth of American and Canadian talent. The Righteous Brothers, the Supremes, Duke Ellington, Eric Burdon and the Animals, and James Brown, to name a few, played there. Today nothing is listed in the Vancouver city directory for the 626 Hornby Street location just west of Georgia, but the HSBC bank office tower occupies the place where that address used to be. In the area is the entrance to the underground parking lot of the HSBC building — a cave of a different kind, perhaps.

On the Cave: "It was my dream to perform in the club one day, and I eventually did in the early '70s. It closed down a few years later as night-clubs became less in vogue but people still talk about the Cave and remember the multitude of wonderful performers who came through. In my opinion, there hasn't been a place since that offers the same variety and quality of good entertainment."
— Susan Jacks, multi-hit singer with the Poppy Family and as a soloist

The Esquire Show Bar

One of Montreal's hottest spots in the 1960s for jazz and blues musicians, the Esquire hosted some of the biggest names in the biz, such as Wilson Pickett. Today, its old Stanley Street location, just south of Ste-Catherine, houses a strip club called Chez Paree.

The Hawk's Nest

Upstairs from the equally legendary Le Coq d'Or on the Yonge Street strip in Toronto, this rocking club was home to Rompin' Ronnie Hawkins and his many band members. Dancing go-go girls and some of the greatest music from the 1960s were featured here. These days the 333 Yonge Street address is home to the main HMV music store in Toronto.

Le Hibou

Le Hibou, Ottawa's legendary Ottawa coffee house, is an integral part of Canadian folk music history. And according to one of its former owners, the club played a role in the formation of one of America's supergroups.

Le Hibou opened in 1961 on the second floor of a two-storey house at 544 Rideau Street, serving coffee and French pastries to customers who took part in chess tournaments, poetry readings, and hootenannies. A year later, co-owner Denis Faulkner moved the club to a commercial building at 248 Bank Street above a paint store where there was more space for entertainment and room to serve more elaborate meals.

It remained there for three years before moving to 521 Sussex Drive, a short stroll east of the Parliament Buildings.

Before Le Hibou closed in 1975, the Sussex Drive location was the gathering place for live music in Ottawa and attracted some of Canada's folk greats, including Joni Mitchell, Ian and Sylvia, Gordon Lightfoot, and Buffy St. Marie. Many American music legends, including John Prine, T-Bone Walker, and Ritchie Havens, also performed at the club.

Harvey Glatt, who co-owned Le Hibou when it was located on Bank Street and Sussex Drive, says

Once a popular Ottawa folk club where music and poetry were on the menu, the original Le Hibou location now serves Indian food.

Ottawa and Le Hibou were at the genesis of American band Crosby, Stills and Nash.

In 1966, Graham Nash and his English pop group the Hollies were appearing at the Capitol Theatre in Ottawa. After their show, Glatt took Nash to Le Hibou, where Joni Mitchell was performing. Later, Glatt, Nash, and Bruce Cockburn visited Mitchell at her Château Laurier hotel room, where the three musicians talked into the night and swapped songs.

"It was clear something was happening between Graham and Joni … there were sparks, so Bruce and I left," recalls Glatt.

Shortly after, Nash left the Hollies, moved to California, and continued his relationship with Mitchell, who introduced him to her good friend David Crosby. Nash and former Byrds member Crosby hit it off, and the rest is history.

"That's how it all started for Crosby, Stills and Nash," says Glatt.

Le Hibou's original Rideau Street location is now an Indian restaurant. The Bank Street venue is a hairdressing salon above a submarine sandwich outlet, and the Sussex Drive location is a clothing store.

On Le Hibou: *"Before The Beatles there were several young fellas at high school who had long hair, not real long, just slightly over the ears. One of the lads was Sandy Crawley, a folkie guitarist. He was also responsible for DRAGGING me to the Le Hibou Coffee House on Bank Street in Ottawa. It changed my life forever, not the drugs, but the music, with lyrics that told stories, none of this moon in June stuff. It was serious."*

— Richard Patterson, drummer, The Esquires and 3's A Crowd

The Riverboat

Located at 134 Yorkville Avenue in Toronto, the Riverboat was arguably the best-known coffee house in Canada. During its years of operation from 1964 to the late 1970s, it featured a who's who of folk music stars, including Gordon Lightfoot, Bruce Cockburn, Joni Mitchell, and Murray McLauchlan. Legend has it that Mitchell's "Clouds" and Phil Ochs's "Changes" were composed in the club's backroom.

The Riverboat is now long gone and is the site of what will be the Hazelton Hotel and Private Residences, eighteen condominium units above a five-star hotel. Before construction began in October 2004, this location was a series of brownstone buildings made up mainly of shops.

On the Riverboat: *"It's why I'm in Toronto to this day. [Music producer and Riverboat manager] Bernie Fielder hired us sight unseen and we came in '65 to play the Riverboat, we got the bug, went home, got our stuff and that was it. The Riverboat in this region was the Mecca."*
— Brent Titcomb, folksinger and actor

The River Heights Community Club
Located on Grosvenor Avenue at Oak Street in the upper-middle-class south Winnipeg neighbourhood of River Heights, this popular music venue opened in the early 1950s and served as a weekend dance hall until the late 1970s.

It was one of about fifty community clubs throughout the city but was seen as the "plum gig" for budding and big-time acts, says John Einarson, a Winnipeg author, broadcaster, and music historian.

Marquis events were always held on Saturdays, often featuring bands

Courtesy of John Einarson

Winnipeg band the Spectres performs at a Saturday night teen dance at the River Heights Community Club in the fall of 1965.

like Chad Allan & the Reflections (later the the Guess Who, who also performed at River Heights), the Deverons with Burton Cummings, the Fifth, the Sugar & Spice, Neil Young & the Squires, and Gettysbyrg Address.

Lineups often formed at five o'clock for a dance that would start three hours later, hosted by such popular deejays as Doc Steen, Ron Legge, Jim Christie, and Bob Burns, host of the TV program *Teen Dance Party*. The club's capacity was four hundred people but more than five hundred sweaty teens would often be shoehorned into the place.

The community centre also had indoor and outdoor hockey rinks, soccer pitches, baseball diamonds, a football field, and a playground area.

The River Heights Community Club is still in operation today and is used for socials and preteen dances and a variety of other community-related activities.

On Neil Young performing at the River Heights Community Club: *"The Squires were one of the most popular bands at River Heights. Neil didn't move around much on stage. His best friend was his amplifier, which he kept close by ... you could tell Neil had confidence in himself as a musician. It wasn't ego or contrived, he was very into the music."*

— Diane Halter, a member of the teen council that booked dances at the River Heights Community Club (taken from *Neil Young: Don't Be Denied — The Canadian Years* by John Einarson)

Courtesy of John Einarson

The River Heights Community Club as it appears today.

Smales Pace

Known in its final incarnation as the Change of Pace, the renowned folk club in London, Ontario, began inauspiciously in the early 1970s as Smales Pace in a converted Bell Canada garage at 436 Clarence Street between Dundas Street and Queens Avenue. Founded by John Smale, the Pace quickly developed a reputation for entertainment and fine food. Several folk musicians such as Stan Rogers, David Wiffen, Doug McArthur, David Bradstreet, and others made their mark there. Rogers was supposed to have written a few songs at the club. In 1976, Smales Pace moved to an upstairs location at 355 Talbot Street, eventually modifying its name to Change of Pace. In 2006 the original location was the site of Nooner's restaurant while the Talbot Street spot was an empty second-floor space available for lease.

Photo by Mark Kearney

David Bradstreet is one of many singer-songwriters who remembers how special Smales Pace folk club was.

On Smales: *"I was no stranger to intimate, outspoken audiences. But Smales Pace was special. The performers were always treated to appreciative audiences and for that, we would have virtually played for nothing, but we always were paid well. It was like coming home each time I was privileged to play there."*

— David Bradstreet, Juno Award–winning singer-songwriter

• • • Bobby Curtola:
Sixties Heartthrob Going Strong

He's in his early sixties, but former teen heartthrob Bobby Curtola can still knock 'em dead. And he's not about to pack away his microphone any day soon.

The native of Port Arthur, Ontario (now Thunder Bay), began singing in choirs and at sock hops at age fourteen and was singing his first hit record on the *Bob Hope Show* by sixteen.

Forty-six years later, he was still performing, on average doing more than fifty shows a year in Canada, the United States, and exotic locales such as Ecuador, Italy, and Malaysia. Now divorced from his wife, Ava, Curtola has lived in an oceanside home in Liverpool, Nova Scotia, since 2004.

In addition to singing, he's a partner in Brandon, Manitoba–based Home Farms Technologies Inc., a high-tech firm that has developed unique processes to manage liquid waste and convert solid waste into energy.

Courtesy of Bobby Curtola

Bobby Curtola as a teen idol in the 1960s.

Fans of Curtola's music are a little older now — moms and dads have replaced the young girls who once swooned at his every move — but his fan base remains strong. Comments found on his website attest to his continued popularity.

"Last night was a great night to be a baby boomer and to be alive," said one fan who attended a Curtola concert in Liverpool in August 2005. "My wife and I attended the Bobby Curtola concert at Seafest along with some friends and it was an evening of excitement to be part of such a great event."

Said another: "The only word I can think of is AWESOME!!!"

Curtola's rise to stardom was nothing short of meteoric. In the fall of 1959 he went from pumping gas at his father's garage to teen idol.

His first hit single, "Hand in Hand with You," was recorded at a radio station in Port Arthur before being released in January 1960. Brothers Basil and Dyer Hurdon, his first managers and songwriters, can be credited for much of this early success.

The hit "Fortune Teller" was released in 1962 and soon went gold in Canada. Curtola then landed a U.S. record deal, and "Fortune Teller" went on to sell 2.5 million copies. The tune broke into the top one hundred in the U.S.

Curtola toured with Dick Clark and his Cavalcade of Stars, and while on tour in England, he met the Beatles and appeared on the popular British TV variety show *Thank Your Lucky Stars*.

Curtola made numerous appearances on network teen TV shows such as *American Bandstand*. His Hollywood debuts were on *Hullabaloo* and *Shindig*. He later hosted two network Canadian TV shows, *After Four* on CFTO in 1965 and 1966 and *Shake, Rock and Roll* on CTV in 1973, as well as a number of Miss Canada and Miss Teen Canada Pageants. In 1969 he opened a show for Louis Armstrong in Toronto.

In the 1960s, he had twenty-five Canadian gold singles, including "Indian Giver," "Three Rows Over," and "Aladdin," and twelve Canadian gold albums, most on the Tartan label. In the mid-1960s he was among Canadian artists who lobbied for Canadian content rules, eventually legislated by the federal government, that guaranteed more Canadian content was seen and heard on radio and TV in Canada.

"Bobby showed people that you can make a good living as an entertainer by staying home … and that you don't have to move somewhere else," says his long-time manager, Robert Hubbard. "He is Canada's rock and roll legend. Nobody has done what Bobby did in the '60s."

In the early 1970s Curtola made the transition from teen idol to nightclub entertainer. Since then he has performed in a variety of venues, including in Las Vegas, where he sang for more than twenty years; on cruise ships; in Malaysia, where he did a Christmas special; and in a string of Hard Rock Cafes, including the one in Bali, Indonesia. He has also sung in Asia, France, Italy, Switzerland, and England. He continues to tour Canada extensively, playing at casinos, sock hop reunions, and special events, some designed to raise money for charity.

In 1975, he married Ava, the daughter of his business agent, and the couple raised two sons, Chris and Michael. The family lived in Edmonton for many years.

He has released a variety of CDs over the years, including in 1990 his *Christmas Flashback* CD, which went gold, and an eight-volume anthology of hits. He expects to release a swing-style album in 2006 or 2007 with Canadian musician/composer/conductor George Blondheim.

Curtola is involved in many charities and has hosted numerous telethons in Canada. His global contributions include charitable works in Indonesia and Bulgaria, the Jerry Lewis Muscular Dystrophy Telethon in the U.S.A., and his Bobby Curtola Foundation for Children in Ecuador.

Curtola received the Order of Canada in 1998 for his humanitarian efforts in Canada and his contribution to Canadian pop music. For his contributions and the establishment of his children's foundation in Ecuador, the Government of Ecuador awarded him the Gold Medal of Merit.

WORTH NOTING…

In June, 1964, Curtola became the first pop singer in North America to record a jingle that sounded like a hit record. The song was "Things Go Better with Coke." Today, it's a common TV-radio advertising ploy to plug products from butter to beer.

• • • The Diamonds:
Harmonizing Through the Decades

Dave Somerville likes to joke that he's spent more than fifty years without a day job.

But that doesn't mean the former member of the Diamonds has spent his career slacking off. In fact, these days he seems to be just as busy as he was in the late 1950s, when the Toronto-based quartet was crooning up the charts with such pop hits as "Little Darlin'," "The Stroll," and "She Say (Oom Dooby Doom)."

When he reflected on his singing career in an early 2006 interview, Somerville had just returned from a week-long gig and was getting ready for another. He had performed on more than a dozen cruises over the past year in such places as the Caribbean and South Africa, playing his solo hits from the 1950s and 1960s. Prior to that he did several reunion gigs with his fellow Diamonds, Phil Levitt, Ted Kowalski, and Bill Reed, that still brought out long-time fans. Some of those shows were PBS television specials that featured the group's tight harmonies, while other performances have come when the Diamonds were inducted into such institutions as the Doo Wop Hall of Fame.

Courtesy of Dave Somerville

Dave Somerville is still singing the Diamonds hits at gigs across North America and beyond.

"I never could have predicted it," he says from his Hollywood home about the longevity of the early rock and roll hits the Diamonds dished out. He recalls touring with Buddy Holly in the late 1950s when both wondered if their music would last even a year. But some fifty years later Somerville says he's as widely recognized as ever because of his link to rock and roll's past. "I'm authentic because I was there," he says.

And the Diamonds were certainly "there" in the 1950s. In an era where vocal groups dominated the airwaves, the Diamonds clearly etched their mark on pop music's history with fifteen Top 40 hits. According to Kowalski, who's a retired electrical engineer in Toronto, the group got its start when he and Levitt were fellow students at the University of Toronto. The two were out doing some surveying when Kowalski saw a pretty co-ed and let out a high-pitched "woooh." Levitt said, "Hey, you sing tenor, don't you?" and soon the two had teamed up with Reed, and shortly thereafter Somerville, for a performance on CBC. Soon, the Diamonds were performing south of the border.

They eventually won a spot on the *Arthur Godfrey Show* and began recording hit singles. Songs such as "Why Do Fools Fall in Love" and "The Church Bells May Ring" on the Mercury label garnered good sales and attention for the group, but it was "Little Darlin'," a cover of a song by the Gladiolas, that rocketed them to fame. They did a little clowning around in the studio singling "la, la, la, las" and adding a spoken part to give the tune a distinctive Diamonds flavour. The song hit number two on Billboard in 1957.

The group managed to keep on the charts until the early 1960s, but eventually the original members left and were replaced by others. Even today, there are a couple of groups in the U.S. called the Diamonds, though none have original members.

For Somerville, the music never stopped. He moved to Hollywood in the 1960s, did commercials and nightclub work, and ended up co-writing the theme song to the TV series *The Fall Guy*. He continues to dabble in various forms of entertainment, offering music on websites for downloading and trying to make deals for a movie or Broadway show. He's still recording CDs and compiling hits of the Diamonds into collections for long-time fans.

As for the other original members, Reed died in late 2004, while Levitt is retired from engineering, living in Toronto, and still doing occasional consulting work. The three remaining members are planning to perform together again.

"I didn't think it would last," Kowalski says of the Diamonds' music, "but the nostalgia era brought it back." And with all the hits the group had, Kowalski has fond memories of singing "You'll Never Walk Alone" when the quartet performed encores in their nightclub act. "It was a different type of harmony from the usual rock and roll ones."

For more information on Dave Somerville, visit diamonddave-somerville.com or diamonddave.tv.

• • • Denny Doherty: Canada's Famous Papa

The legend of the Mamas & the Papas lives on thanks to Denny Doherty, Canada's representative in the popular U.S.–based folk pop foursome that produced a string of memorable hit records in the 1960s.

For several years, the son of a Halifax pipefitter, whose mellow voice was at the core of such successful hits as "California Dreamin'" and "Monday, Monday," has performed the stage production *Dream a Little Dream, the nearly true story of the Mamas & the Papas*, a one-person show backed by a six-piece band.

The two-hour narrative, written by Doherty, has been staged in many American and Canadian cities, including New York City, Halifax, Missouri, and Kansas City.

"It was a challenge to put together," says Doherty, now in his mid-sixties. "I had to compress 40 years into two hours."

In 2006, Doherty was hopeful the show would evolve into a full-blown stage production performed by theatre groups on Broadway and at other live venues. Doherty wasn't planning on acting or singing in the show but hoped to work with Michelle Phillips, another former member of the Mamas & the Papas, as a consultant to ensure the product is true to life.

Doherty joined the Mamas & the Papas in the mid-1960s after bouncing between a number of bands, including the Hepsters, the Journeymen, the Big Three, and the Mugwumps.

Images of former band mate Michelle Phillips and Denny Doherty's insight are part of a play written and performed by Doherty that remembers the short-lived career of the Mamas & the Papas.

Courtesy of Ken Kam

Other members of the harmony-rich group were John Phillips, Michelle Phillips, and Cass Elliot. The southern California–based foursome had three gold albums and a number of hit singles, and along the way rubbed shoulders with dozens of music industry icons, including John Sebastian and Zal Yanovsky of the Lovin' Spoonful, Barry McGuire, John Lennon, Simon and Garfunkel, and Ravi Shankar.

When the Mamas & the Papas split up in 1968, Doherty lived in New York for several years and appeared in a number of plays. He returned to Halifax in 1977 and hosted a series of CBC variety shows and toured the Maritimes with the Neptune Theatre.

In 1974, Cass Elliot travelled to England, where, in July, at the age of thirty-three, she died of a heart attack.

In 1982, with the nostalgia kick going strong, Doherty went back on the road with a new version of the Mamas & the Papas, which included original member John Phillips, who had recently cleaned up his act after running into trouble with drugs; his daughter, Mackenzie Phillips of *One Day at a Time* TV show fame; and Elaine "Spanky" McFarlane, who'd sung with U.S. pop group Spanky and Our Gang back in the 1960s.

John died of heart failure in 2001. Michelle Phillips continues to sing and act in the U.S.

Doherty has lived in Mississauga, Ontario, since 1986, where he continues to write songs he hopes to record and perform. His wife, Jeanette, passed away in the mid-1980s, and the singer underwent a double heart bypass in January 2004. He has two children, Emberley and John, both in their mid-twenties. John is a member of Ill Scarlett, a contemporary rock band.

Since the late 1980s, much of Doherty's life has involved work in the theatre, including playing the role of preacher J.D. Blackwell in the production *Fire*, a play that examined the theme of rock and roll versus the church. He has also spent considerable time raising his family after many years on the road.

"It got to the point where I was away too much, my kids didn't know who I was," he said after leaving the new Mamas & the Papas.

The original band's hits, including "California Dreamin'," "Monday Monday," "Dedicated to the One I Love," "I Saw Her Again Last Night," and "I Call Your Name," are still played regularly on the radio.

• • • Edward Bear: No Last (Swan) Song

In an era when seemingly every rock band from the 1960s and 1970s has reunited at least once for a final blast of glory, Edward Bear remains an exception.

Although band members of the former chart-topping Toronto group have received overtures over the years about getting back together, it just hasn't happened. There are many reasons, but lead singer and drummer Larry Evoy has his theory.

"It has to be this complete, whole magical thing or it's not worth doing," he says from his home in King City, Ontario. He's wondered what format such a reunion would take, where it would be, why the band should do it, and what kind of music to even play. The original members, along with Evoy, were guitarist Danny Marks and keyboard player Paul Weldon. But Marks left the band around 1971 just as it was having chart success and Weldon moved on a year later. Other players replaced them, and Evoy wonders what version of Edward Bear would even do such a concert.

The original version of the band was heavier and played harder edged rock, Evoy says, noting that in those days Edward Bear opened for Led Zeppelin. But the band is better known for its pop side, with such hits as "You, Me and Mexico," "Last Song," "Masquerade," and "Close Your Eyes."

For his part, Evoy hasn't been much involved in music in recent years and isn't feeling motivated to get back into it. He doesn't miss the fan appreciation and he's not keen to go back on the road again for long-term gigs or to get serious about it. "For me it was always goofy fun."

Marks also enjoys the fun side of music and has carved a niche in Canada as one of the most versatile players around. He left Edward Bear early on because he didn't want to be a guy who ended up having his peak experience in his twenties. "I was really proud of what we'd done," he says, but for him it was time to move on. Marks has probably maintained the highest profile of any of the members. His regular appearances with the Hum Line segment of CBC Radio's "Basic Black" as well as the many gigs he's played in and around Toronto have kept him in the public eye.

Thanks to radio and the gigs, Marks had a reputation in the 1980s and 1990s as "the human jukebox." His repertoire seemed almost endless.

During an interview for this book, Marks mentioned how he had just realized the night before that he knew how to play and sing the old Faron Young tune "Funny Face" and began singing a few lines.

In addition to performing, Marks has appeared in some movies, one starring Omar Sharif, and has written some music articles. In 2006, he was the host of a Saturday night blues show, BLUZ.FM, on Toronto jazz station CJRT. He's also released four CDs in recent years, the most recent *Big Town Boy*, which draws mostly on Toronto radio hits from 1963 to 1965. "You, Me and Mexico" is also included on the album. "I felt it was important to address my past," Marks once told an interviewer. "It's a beautiful song." His other albums are *Guitarchaeology* (1997) *Surfin' Safari* (1999), and *True* (2003). He still performs occasionally, including in the U.S. and Finland, and hopes to do more live gigs in the future.

Like Evoy, Marks is not sure if an Edward Bear reunion is a good idea. "I can see how it's intriguing to insiders and outsiders," he says, but he believes a reunion can look like "we've run out of stuff." Weldon, however, says he'd be up for it if the idea ever got off the ground.

Photo by Mark Kearney

He sang "Freedom for the Stallion," and Larry Evoy is still keeping busy raising horses.

Evoy did get a chance to sing briefly at a 2000 concert that brought together new and older artists. Calling it the best gig of his life because it was short and easy, Evoy says he'd be interested in a reunion if the pieces fell together. He's in touch with Weldon, who teaches graphic arts part-time at Centennial College, and works in sales for Stanford Design, also in Toronto. Weldon also plays regularly in a jazz group called the T.O. Trio.

For the most part, Evoy is content to spend time at

his fifty-two-acre, cottage-like home north of Toronto, where he and his wife, Sara, raise and show horses. In his post–Edward Bear days, he's also dabbled in theatre and comedy performing. Like other musicians with solid hits, Evoy receives a steady stream of royalties thanks to compilation CDs and consistent airplay of his songs on oldies stations around North America. He's noticed lately that "Close Your Eyes," which was a smaller hit for Edward Bear, seems to be getting attention.

"I don't know," he says with a laugh. "Maybe they got sick of playing 'Last Song.'"

For more information on Danny Marks, visit his website at www.dannym.com.

• • • Les Emmerson: Life Is Absolutely Right

Once a rocker, always a rocker — and as time marches on, a golfer and trivia buff, too.

That's how life is shaping up for veteran Ottawa musician and song-writer Les Emmerson, a member of Ottawa groups the Staccatos and Five Man Electrical Band.

Between the mid-1960s and early 1970s, Emmerson wrote or sang dozens of hits for both bands, including "Half Past Midnight," "I'm a Stranger Here," "Absolutely Right," and "Signs," an anti-establishment anthem that sold more than 1.5 million copies and has since sold millions more records for two other bands, including American rock group Tesla.

Known initially as Dean Hagopian and the Staccatos, the group formed in Ottawa in 1963. Its sound was rock with a hint of country and plenty of harmony. Members came and went and the name was eventually shortened to the Staccatos. In 1979 they became Five Man Electrical Band, the title of a song written by Emmerson.

Emmerson and his bandmates had a string of musical milestones: in 1967, the Staccatos were picked Canadian group of the year and played for Queen Elizabeth in Ottawa. They recorded the LP *A Wild Pair* with the Guess Who in a unique promotion for Coca-Cola. In total, the band released six albums.

In its heyday, Five Man Electrical Band performed with a variety of big-name acts, including the James Gang, Paul Butterfield, J. Geils, Humble Pie, and Bread.

In 1974, its members tired of touring and headed in different musical directions, Five Man Electrical Band split. Emmerson later had solo hit singles "Control of Me" and "Cry Your Eyes Out," which he recorded in California before returning to Canada in 1981.

Five Man Electrical Band reunited for a show in Ottawa in 1986 and the original lineup later played several other concerts together.

Now in his early sixties, Emmerson continues to perform as part of a new version of the band in a lineup that includes original members keyboardist Ted Gerow and drummer Mike Belanger and new additions drummer/singer Steve Hollingworth, singer/guitarist Ross McRae, and bassist/singer Rick Smithers.

The current version plays about ten concerts a year. After visiting California in January 2006, the group was being considered for inclusion in a music documentary highlighting bands from the 1960s and 1970s. In the spring of 2006, the band played a handful of West Coast concert dates.

Emmerson also leads Les Emmerson & the Hitmen, which performs mainly in Ottawa, usually doing Five Man Electrical Band and Staccatos songs, as well as tunes by other groups. He has an album's worth of songs in his head and hopes to record some under the Five Man name.

"It's the Five Man sound, good old rock and roll with lots of harmony," he says.

He's married to Monik and has a teenage daughter, Kristina. They live in the suburbs of Ottawa, where he's on the links three times a week when he's not playing and writing music.

"I am obsessed with the game of golf," says Emmerson, who's involved in a trivia league in Ottawa and loves to play electronic trivia at local pubs. "My wife got me into golf one father's day with golf shoes and some clubs. For an old, lazy music guy, it's great to be able to play during the week when the courses aren't crowded."

Courtesy of Les Emmerson

Les Emmerson, centre, with the modern version of Ottawa-based Five Man Electrical Band.

Brian Rading, Five Man Electrical Band's former bass player, is a home renovator in Ottawa. Drummer Rick Belanger (Mike Belanger's brother) lives in Toronto where he installs wiring for a computer company.

WORTH NOTING...

"Signs," Five Man Electrical Band's biggest hit, was written by Emmerson "as an afterthought" in 1971 on a piece of paper in his guitar case. "We were driving along a highway in the U.S. and there were advertising signs everywhere. I thought, 'what a shame to cover up this lovely country.'"

• • • Susan Jacks: Knows Which Way She's Goin'

Some of the teachers who helped Susan Jacks negotiate her way through elementary and high school weren't impressed when she decided on a career as an entertainer.

"I think many thought I was wasting my brain … they didn't think I'd go too far," says Jacks, a former member of 1960s and 1970s pop group the Poppy Family. "I'll bet they're pretty pleased with me now."

No doubt about that.

While performing with former husband Terry Jacks, Susan helped the Poppy Family sell more than 5 million records with such hits as "Which Way You Goin' Billy?," "Good Friends," and "That's Where I Went Wrong." In the early 1970s, Terry made the decision to stop recording as the Poppy Family and Terry and Susan began making records separately, while continuing to work together in the studio.

They co-produced her album *I Thought of You Again* and several other songs, including Terry's hit "Seasons in the Sun," before their marriage ended in 1973.

Susan recorded a handful of solo singles and LPs, including *Forever and Ghosts*, before moving to Nashville in 1983. Her singles "Tall Dark Stranger," "I Thought of You Again," "Anna Marie," and "All the Tea in China" received Juno nominations. "Tall Dark Stranger" won her Best New Female Country Artist honours in Oklahoma in 1984.

Jacks, who was born Susan Pesklevits in Saskatoon in 1948 and began singing at age seven, has also scored considerable success outside of music.

Although singing and songwriting remained an integral part of her life after she moved to Tennessee, where she was a staff songwriter for a publishing company for five years, she also developed a career in business.

With her second husband, Ted Dushinski, a former Canadian Football League defensive back, she ran a storefront perogi outlet; she later managed a publishing company and was vice-president of operations for a computer consulting company. More recently, Jacks was an owner and executive vice-president of a successful telecommunications company in Nashville.

After living in the Nashville area for more than twenty years, Jacks's life took an abrupt turn in 2004 when she returned to Canada to help

Dushinski, also a native of Saskatoon, deal with lung cancer. The disease took his life at age sixty-one in October 2005 in New Westminster, B.C.

"We had been apart for eleven years but we were still very close friends," says Jacks. "I didn't want him to go through the disease alone. Ultimately, I asked if he would be okay with us going back home and he really wanted to do that so we moved to Vancouver. His last year was filled with wonderful things ... he was back in touch with his football friends and members of his family and my family."

In 2006, Jacks was in her late fifties and was living in Port Roberts, Washington, a short drive south of the Canada–U.S. border, where she was chief operations officer of Solara Technologies, a company that develops remote management technology for vending machines and kiosks, and is also in the field of transaction processing and digital signage.

With company president Dorn Beattie, the former lead singer of West Coast band Painter, she was developing a new branch of the firm, which would include an independent record label to produce and distribute CDs for up-and-coming artists, who are often shunned by large labels.

The company also hopes to work with artists who don't necessarily have a chance to get on the airwaves because they don't fit the look, sound, or age that major labels are looking for.

"I come from an era when you could be good and have a chance, and you could make it. Now, artists have little chance of getting anywhere, often because they are eaten up with expenses charged by the major labels," says Jacks, whose twenty-eight-year-old son, Thad, lives in

Courtesy of Susan Jacks

Susan Jacks as a young singer in the 1970s. She's back on the West Coast after living in Nashville for many years.

Nashville. "They rarely get their money back and the big companies drop them in a heartbeat if they do not meet ridiculous criteria for record sales. We want to empower artists, rather than control them."

If all goes well, Jacks, with Beattie's help as an investor and his experience in the entertainment industry, will produce and record artists at a studio in Port Coquitlam, just outside of Vancouver, and other studios as needed.

"I've produced in some of the best studios in the world and a good sound and good engineer are a must," she says.

Although her music career has had its ups and downs over the years — including being ripped off for $150,000 by a former manager — she's confident her latest venture will be successful. She also hopes to record some of the songs she wrote in Nashville and others she has written since returning to Vancouver.

"I lost confidence over the years, I admit that. But my corporate work has helped me regain my confidence and Ted's battle with cancer helped me build up another kind of strength that will help in the future."

WORTH NOTING...

Susan Jacks first sang professionally at age fourteen at a legion dance in Haney, B.C., for which she was paid $1. At fifteen, she became a regular performer on the national Canadian TV show *Music Hop*, where she met Terry Jacks, whose band, the Chessman, was performing on the program. Later, when Susan was asked to sing in Hope, B.C., Terry agreed to accompany her on guitar and they began performing together, eventually taking the name the Poppy Family. Susan and Terry married in 1967.

• • • Terry Jacks:
The Environment Is Now His Bestseller

In the mid-1970s, Terry Jacks scored international acclaim with the song "Seasons in the Sun," which has sold more than 13 million copies worldwide, making it the biggest selling single recorded by a Canadian artist.

"Not everyone remembers me but people remember the song," Jacks said from his home on British Columbia's Sunshine Coast, three hours north of Vancouver.

Since making a name for himself in the music industry, initially as a member of Vancouver band the Chessmen, later with former wife Susan in the Poppy Family, and finally as a solo artist, music has been on the back burner for Jacks for nearly two decades.

The environment has been his true passion since the mid-1980s when his daughter Holly was born, although he's been dabbling in music in recent years.

"When my daughter arrived we had to close the windows of our home because the smell from nearby pulp mills was so bad," says Jacks. "We were living on Howe Sound near Vancouver, about fifteen miles away from the mills, and we asked ourselves 'why do we have to put up with this, the air and water belong to all of us.'"

Courtesy of Terry Jacks

And after learning that pulp and paper companies were not complying with their government permits, Jacks began dedicating long hours to raising public awareness about how the pulp and paper industry was threatening the West Coast environment. Soon after, the waters of Howe Sound were closed to fishing because of contamination from the mills.

Terry Jacks still sings and writes songs, but the environment is at the top of his agenda.

He founded the West Coast environmental network Environmental Watch, helped fishermen and boaters organize protests, made presentations to legislators in B.C., took a former B.C. environment minister and a pulp and paper company to court, fought applications by pulp and paper companies to increase emissions, and produced several award-winning documentaries that, among other things, show how the B.C. forest industry for years has put economics ahead of the environment.

One of his videos won two awards at the New York International Film Festival; Jacks also received an award from the United Nations for his environmental efforts, which was presented by the Western Canada Wilderness Committee. In 1992, he received the first Eugene Rogers Award for his work to stop pulp mill pollution on the B.C. coast. The award is named after a New Westminster, B.C., conservationist who fought to protect the province's wild places and wild salmon.

"The purpose of the video was to let people know what is going on and how the government and industry were in bed together ... individuals hide within governments and corporations and are able to escape being held personally responsible for their actions. Thus the title of the video, the *Faceless Ones*."

Jacks was born in Winnipeg in 1944, where he decided on a music career after abandoning potential careers in architecture and professional golf. His first band was the Chessmen, which released four singles. He played rhythm guitar, wrote the songs, and sang lead.

In the late 1960s, he linked up with Susan Pesklevits, later his first wife, to form the Poppy Family, a moniker he found in the dictionary. The group released about a dozen records, including *Which Way You Goin' Billy?* which sold 3 million copies and hit number one on *Cashbox* in the United States. Other hits included "That's Where I Went Wrong" and "Where Evil Grows." The group sold more than 5 million records.

The Poppy Family stopped performing in 1971, and shortly after that the Jacks's marriage collapsed. Terry and Susan then embarked on solo careers.

"Seasons in the Sun" was Terry's first major hit. In 1974, the song won a Juno Award for Best Contemporary/Pop Single and Jacks won another Juno for Best Male Vocalist. A year later, "Seasons in the Sun" won the Juno for bestselling single for the second year in a row, a

Canadian first. Jacks's other hits included "If You Go Away" and "Concrete Sea."

In the mid-1970s, Jacks remarried, stepped out of the music industry spotlight, and turned his attention to the environment. At one point, he didn't touch his guitar for five years. In 1981, he co-produced, starred in, and wrote all the music for a television movie called *Seasons in the Sun*, a spy story released only in Europe.

Since returning to his musical roots, Jacks has released a chronological CD compilation of all the Poppy Family tunes called *A Good Thing Lost*, with liner notes that explain why each song was written. His production and publishing company is Gone Fishin' Music Ltd. He has been producing and arranging a CD for singer-songwriter/guitar player Jana Keeley, who he believes will be a major artist.

In recent years Jacks has performed live and on television in Germany, Norway, England, and the Netherlands. In 2005, he was inducted to the B.C. Music Hall of Fame, along with Randy Bachman, also a Winnipeg native.

While in Europe he met with environment ministers to express his concerns about various issues, including threats to the world's whale population and the continuous clear-cutting of the ancient forests in B.C.

He lives alone in his oceanside home and spends much of his free time on his boat. Now in his early sixties, Jacks underwent surgery for prostate cancer in March of 2006.

WORTH NOTING...

The song "Seasons in the Sun" was originally called "Le Moribond," written by a friend of Jacks's, French singer-songwriter Jacques Brel. Its original tongue-in-cheek lyrics related the story of a man dying of a broken heart because his wife was cheating on him with his best friend. It was translated to English by Rod McKuen, and Jacks rewrote the song after one of his good friends passed away. "He told me on the golf course that he had acute leukemia, with no cure. He said he had not yet told his father or his girlfriend." He died four months later.

• • • Pierre Juneau:
The Name Behind the Juno Awards

The Canadian music industry's Juno Awards are named after Pierre Juneau, and with good reason.

During a distinguished forty-year career with the National Film Board, the Board of Broadcast Governors (later the Canadian Radio-television and Telecommunications Commission), the federal government, and the Canadian Broadcasting Corporation, he was known as Canada's "culture czar" for his efforts to preserve and protect Canadian content in radio and television broadcasting.

In 1966, after seventeen years as an administrator with NFB, including two years as European representative and four years as director of French production, the native of Verdun, Quebec, was appointed vice-chairman of the Board of Broadcast Governors, which regulated and supervised all aspects of Canadian broadcasting. When the BBG became the CRTC in 1968, he became its first chairman.

While with the CRTC, he presided over the Canadianization of all large cable TV companies operating in Canada and several important television and radio companies, which until then were under British or American ownership.

In the early 1970s, Juneau was one of the architects of the CRTC's Canadian content regulations, which required that no less than 30 percent of music programmed on radio stations had to be produced in Canada. The rules also ensured that 60 percent of prime-time television programming was Canadian.

By requiring radio stations to give airplay to Canadian artists, the regulations are credited with creating a domestic market for Canadian music and the subsequent boom in music production. For his efforts, the music industry's Juno Awards, which marked their thirty-fifth anniversary in 2006, were named after Juneau. Previously they were known as the RPM Gold Leaf Awards.

"At the time, everyone in the music industry, composers, singers and small companies, was having a hard time," says Juneau. "With the new content regulations we witnessed an event that was quite moving for the industry. There were hardly any recording studios in Canada back then. People would go to the United States to record. Now, Canada has studios all over the place."

Juneau served as CRTC chairman until 1975, when he accepted an appointment by Prime Minister Pierre Trudeau as minister of communications. Since he did not have a seat in the House of Commons, he attempted to enter Parliament through a by-election but was defeated in the Montreal riding of Hochelaga by the Progressive Conservative candidate. He resigned from cabinet.

He was subsequently appointed to the civil service by Trudeau as undersecretary of state, and then, in 1980, as deputy minister of communications.

In 1982, he became president of the Canadian Broadcasting Corporation and held the post until 1989. Despite financial pressures during his term, Juneau inaugurated a new cable service, CBC Newsworld, and increased Canadian content on the CBC to 85 percent of programming.

He is an officer of the Order of Canada and in 2005 was inducted into the Canadian Music Hall of Fame.

Now a resident of Montreal and in his mid-eighties, Juneau is on the board of the Canadian Consortium for Research in the Media. He spends most of his spare time playing tennis, gardening, and reading. He and Fernande, his wife of sixty years, also spend as much time as possible with their three children and eight grandchildren.

Courtesy of Pierre Juneau

Pierre Juneau helped bring Canadian content to the forefront. He now lives in Montreal.

• • • Klaatu: A Long and Winding Road

John Woloschuk of Klaatu says every story he's ever read about the band mentions the connection of his group to the Beatles. So let's get right to it. One of the reasons Klaatu still generates interest to this day is that

In the mid-1970s Klaatu had the world thinking they were the Beatles reunited.

back in the mid-1970s the Toronto-based trio was mistakenly thought to be the Beatles secretly reunited.

The rumours first hit when a Rhode Island journalist played Klaatu's first album and was convinced it was the Fab Four of Liverpool who had clandestinely gotten together to make a record. The fact that the album jacket provided no names, credits, or song titles only added to the mystery. There were several other "clues" unearthed, and the rumours "spread like a grass fire," says Woloschuk. "That's what it was like."

Klaatu was in the middle of recording its second album for Capitol Records, which seemed content to do nothing to squelch the rumours. Says Woloschuk, "It was almost a distraction. [But] it was flattering to be compared to the Beatles."

Eventually, however, the world found out the true nature of the band and the blame, such as it was, fell on Klaatu's members. "It's the kiss of death to be compared to the Beatles," he says, noting that British band Badfinger also suffered similar comparisons. It didn't stop Klaatu from continuing to record and perform, landing a couple of songs on the Canadian charts, including "Knee Deep in Love" and "Dear Christine," and hitting it big financially when the Carpenters recorded a version of "Calling Occupants."

But Terry Draper, another Klaatu member, says today the trio still suffers the slings and arrows of criticism simply for doing the kind of music they loved. "We were good enough to be the Beatles playing, but under our name you should be able to have a career in the industry. And we were denied that."

The band continued to record and eventually each member's name was revealed. Some touring followed, but nothing could match the interest generated when everyone thought of them as the Beatles. For most of the 1980s the band members went their own way. Draper operated a roofing business in Oak Ridges, north of Toronto, while still keeping his hands in music; the other member of the trio, Dee Long, had his own recording studio; and Woloschuk became a certified general accountant and set up a successful practice in Toronto that he continues to this day. "[Accounting] satisfies my need to do something worthwhile," he said in an interview. He also looks after the Klaatu catalogue and, with a strong international following, the band's royalties still flow in. "Calling Occupants" is one of the big revenue generators.

As for Draper, he gave up the roofing business ("a young man's job") and has dabbled in various projects including owning a bar, bartending, and in early 2006 working as something of a comptroller in a nightclub in Vaughan, Ontario. "The whole bar world is a comfort zone for me," he says, having played in them since he was a young man. Draper, who has a studio in his basement, has also released a few solo CDs and enjoys jamming with his wife, who plays violin and cello. Long moved to British Columbia and has recorded from his home studio there, including his animated DVD *Outside of Time & Space*. Bullseye Records released his live CD *Live Long & Prosper* (recorded in 2005 at the Brunswick House in Toronto) and his next studio album was set for release in 2006.

Klaatu fans, meanwhile, were treated to a mini-reunion of sorts when the three members gathered at a conference in Toronto in May 2005 to perform a few songs and meet their fans, some of whom travelled from outside Canada to be there. During the band's first rehearsal it felt like the three of them had been apart for only two weeks, says Draper, while Woloschuk said their performance was "better than what you'd think" given that it had been many years since the trio had performed together. "Judging by the fans' reaction we managed to pull it off."

Though there were no plans for another reunion, Klaatu remains an important part of many fans around the world for their musical style, which saw them try all kinds of different genres to achieve a unique sound. The casual observer may still think "Beatles" when the trio's name comes up, but serious fans see it only as footnote, Woloschuk says. "I've been struck by how loyal the fans have been."

To learn more about Klaatu's career and songs visit klaatu.org.

• • • Don Messer's Violin:
The Torch Has Been Passed

Many of Canada's most prized artifacts have disappeared. Others, for lack of proper display space, are hidden in storerooms where Canadians may never see or touch them.

The violin played by the late Canadian music legend Don Messer is an exception: it's under the stewardship of Canadian fiddle champion Frank Leahy of Teeswater, Ontario, who plays it on a regular basis and occasionally lets other fiddle players take their turn with the bow.

Leahy acquired the prized instrument in 1997, twenty-four years after Messer's death. It's the same French-made violin that Messer used during thousands of live shows and barn dances, on the radio, and on his popular television folk music variety show, *Don Messer's Jubilee*, which was produced at station CBHT in Halifax, Nova Scotia, and broadcast by the CBC network nationwide from 1958 until 1969.

The half-hour weekly program featured Don Messer and His Islanders, including singers Marg Osburne and Charlie Chamberlain as well as a guest performer.

Courtesy of Frank Leahy

Frank Leahy of Waterloo, Ontario, is custodian of the prized violin that was played by Don Messer on television and radio and during live performances.

Outside of *Hockey Night in Canada*, in the mid-1960s *Don Messer's Jubilee* was the number one show in the country, sometimes earning higher ratings than CBS's *The Ed Sullivan Show*. The cancellation of the show by the public broadcaster in 1969 caused a nationwide protest, with even members of Parliament in the House of Commons raising questions.

Messer, a native of Tweedside, New Brunswick, died of a heart attack on March 26, 1973. Following the death of his wife, Naomi, a few years later, the Messers' three daughters divvied up their father's collection of instruments, with eldest daughter Dawn Attis getting *the* violin. After it sat in her closet in Halifax for more than twenty years, its strings decaying and its bridge in disrepair, Attis decided it was time to pass the instrument on to a fiddle player of this generation.

Looking at the case, she could almost hear her father's voice saying, "a good instrument needs to be played," author Li Robbins wrote in her book *Don Messer's Violin: Canada's Fiddle.*

After interviewing several fiddlers, Attis picked Leahy, who had never met Messer but had admired and was influenced by his music since he first picked up a violin at the age of six. Prior to being contacted by Attis, Leahy had no idea the violin still existed.

"Dawn interviewed me in a series of four phone calls and I was chosen to carry on what Don did for all of those years," says Leahy, who lives in Waterloo, Ontario, and keeps the instrument in a humidity-controlled case. "To what do I compare the feeling of being picked? It was like when I was watching the 1987 Canada Cup when Gretzky passed the puck to Lemieux and he scored that big goal. I still can't believe it has happened."

Since then, Leahy, whose repertoire is a mix of classical, country, swing, and jazz, has used the violin at numerous concerts in North America and on a half-dozen CDs he has produced, including *Don Messer's Violin*, which was released in 2000, the same year he co-wrote, produced, and starred in the musical *Don Messer's Violin*, which had a three-year run on Prince Edward Island.

Leahy has collaborated with violinist Edward Minevich for more than one hundred Symphony Pops concerts and recently teamed up with virtuoso violinist Robin Braun for a new Symphony Pops show entitled *An Unlikely Affair.*

At shows where he plays Messer's songs on Messer's violin, members of the audience often break down in tears. Following most of his concerts, he invites fiddlers in the crowd to play a few tunes on the instrument.

"To this day the power of Don's violin is incredible," says Leahy. "It is unbelievable how it affects people."

• • • RPM: Serving Music, Then Meals

RPM Magazine was long the bible of Canadian music, thanks to the work and vision of Walter Grealis and Stan Klees. The offices at 6 Brentcliffe Road in Toronto turned out the trade magazine from 1964 until 2000, paralleling the rise of Canadian music to the point where performers from this country are now well known and respected around the world.

Grealis and Klees were highly vocal supporters of Canadian talent, an especially key element in the mid-1960s when few radio stations and record labels were paying attention to homegrown talent. *RPM* inaugurated the Gold Leaf Awards, the precursor to the Juno Awards of today, and lobbied the CRTC to bring in the controversial Canadian content regulations that forced radio stations to play a certain amount of Canadian music daily. A Juno Award in Grealis's name was established in 1984.

The *RPM* MAPL logo found on singles and albums was designed by Klees to identify the Canadian content based on music's composer, artist, production, and lyrics, although to his chagrin, some have questioned his role in this.

Photo by Mark Kearney

Once home of Canada's music industry bible, RPM's former location is now a café.

RPM Magazine closed down in November 2000, and the building was turned into a café in 2003 that was run in 2006 by Costa Bellas and is open seven days a week. Decorating the café's walls are old issues of *RPM* and memorabilia.

Grealis learned in 2000 that he had cancer, and Klees says, "I spent the next three years looking after Walt." Both men agreed to walk away completely from the industry that they had lived and breathed for decades.

Grealis died on January 20, 2004, passing away in Klees's home peacefully "after he asked for all life support to be disconnected."

Since then Klees has kept busy speaking to students in colleges on Cancon, radio, the music business, theatre, public relations, motivation, and cultural colonization. Klees also travels, making a couple of transatlantic cruises every year and visiting southern Europe whenever possible. And in what is perhaps a fitting connection to his earlier career, Klees also lunches most Fridays at the RPM Café.

Klees leaves the last word about the duo's long uphill battle to establish and strengthen Canadian music to Grealis, who said in 1999, "The record business in Canada is based on kindness, sincerity and integrity. Once you learn to fake all three, you've got it made."

• • • Ken Tobias:
He Still Just Wants to Make Music

Thirty-five years of writing songs, several of them hits, haven't dulled Ken Tobias's passion for music.

Speaking from Saint John, New Brunswick, his hometown to which he returned to live in July 2004 after three decades in Toronto, Tobias has excitement in his voice as he talks about his new material. He recites lyrics from some of the tunes, mentioning how he writes more directly now, instead of trying to be oblique.

"In the past when I wasn't feeling great I'd write an 'up' song ... but if I don't feel great now I write it down," he says with a chuckle. "I'm very happy with the way I'm writing now."

And while his long-time fans still cheer when he plays hits such as "Every Bit of Love," "Dream # 2," and "I Just Want to Make Music," he's finding that when he performs these days fans also embrace the new material. He's putting out his first record since 1984 and looking forward to touring with it if possible.

Although Tobias may have had a lower profile since his heyday in the 1970s, he's always been writing music, including soundtracks, and performing from time to time. But a return to his Maritime roots seems to have energized him. He says he's surprised by how he can't walk the streets of Saint John without people warmly welcoming him back. "They say 'glad to have you back, Kenny (they call me Kenny). You're still a Maritimer, man.' I get up [on stage] and thank them. It almost brings tears to my eyes."

An even more tearful song-related event took place in 2003 when Tobias heard that a long-time fan of his was dying of cancer. Apparently the British Columbia man loved playing Tobias's "Dream # 2" over and over to the point that he wore the record out. When the man's sister contacted Tobias about the news of the cancer, the singer-songwriter called him up, chatted for awhile, and sent a CD with the song on it.

The man listened to it and died shortly afterwards. When the sister contacted Tobias with the news, the singer "sobbed for about 20 minutes. I was part of something, you know. His last two hours on earth were happy because of the song. That's what it's all about."

Not that Tobias's career has been without highlights. He has some 285 songs registered with SOCAN and several of them have been acknowledged as being played on the radio more than one hundred thousand times. Tobias wrote the hit single "Stay Awhile" for the Bells, became a protegé of sorts of Bill Medley of the Righteous Brothers, and hung out with Phil Everly before launching his successful solo career in Canada. His songs still get extensive radio airplay across the country, but he admits that critics sometimes seem to overlook his accomplishments when they talk of Canadian musicians from that era. "I'm not trying to get something, but it's like I've fallen through the cracks," he says.

But Tobias is enjoying performing and writing these days, collaborating with a young singer-songwriter named Jessica Rhaye. He describes his new material as "funkier" than before, but says that he's still "a good hook guy; I write good hooks." When he's not writing or playing, he has a second career as an artist, selling his mostly acrylic paintings in galleries in Toronto and to private collectors for as much as $2,500.

He admits that in his early years he was more nervous about performing but that he's now comfortable because of his experience. "I really dig it," he says, and the enthusiasm in his voice is obvious.

Want to know more about what Ken Tobias is up to these days? Visit his website at www.kentobias.ca.

Courtesy of Craig Stephen

Ken Tobias has returned to his Maritime roots where he still writes songs and performs.

• • • First Music Video: Still Rocking

A film showing early 1960s Ottawa band the Esquires playing two of their songs is thought to be Canada's first rock and roll music video.

"It is probably the first video made with the purpose of promoting the group and not just a copy of a TV or concert appearance," says Richard Green, who is acting manager of the Music Section, Library and Archives Canada.

The footage was filmed in Ottawa in 1964 for use in a novelty juke-box known as the "Scopeotone" that incorporated a movie screen.

When the machines were first imported to Canada from Europe by Regent Vending of Ottawa, the films showed mainly Italian and French singers. It was later decided that Canadian talent would be more appro-priate, so a camera crew and Ottawa film company did the filming on a set built by Ottawa TV station CJOH.

On the film, the Esquires play two of their songs, "Man From Adano" and "Gee Whiz It's You." The two-minute film could be seen in

Courtesy of Richard Patterson

The Esquires perform on what is believed to be Canada's first music video, which is in storage in Ottawa.

jukeboxes in Ottawa and Hull (now Gatineau), which is located in Quebec across the Ottawa River from the nation's capital.

The machines and the Esquires video eventually disappeared. The videos resurfaced when a fire in an Ottawa warehouse destroyed everything but a trunk containing film canisters that had been in storage for nearly twenty years.

After being recovered, the film was sent to the National Archives of Canada (now Library and Archives Canada) in Ottawa, where it was cleaned and restored and remains part of the Archives' audiovisual collection. Richard Patterson, drummer for the Esquires, also has a copy.

The video has been shown on MuchMusic, where host Terry David Mulligan declared that it was likely the first professional music video produced by a Canadian band.

The original film, part of the Regent Vending and Amusement Ltd. collection and entitled *Gee Whiz It's You*, is in storage at the Archives' Gatineau Preservation Centre in Gatineau, Quebec. A VHS copy (Reference No. v1 2003-12-0018) can be viewed at the Library and Archives Canada building at 395 Wellington Street in Ottawa.

BITS AND PIECES
• • •
Objects of Our Past Affection

• • • The *Bluenose*: Sailing into History

The *Bluenose*, a Canadian icon and easily Canada's most famous ship, was launched with much fanfare at Lunenburg, Nova Scotia, in 1921.

When she began plying the waters off the east coast of North America, fishing vessels in the Maritime provinces and the New England states were well-built sailing ships that could weather the rigorous challenges of the North Atlantic fishing, sail speedily, and hold large cargoes of fish.

Bluenose, designed by William J. Roué of Halifax, was no different.

As a racing ship, she was skippered by Captain Angus J. Walters against some of the speediest American schooners in races for the International Fishermen's Trophy, an annual competition established by the *Halifax Herald* newspaper after years of friendly rivalry between bona fide working fishing schooners from the United States and Canada.

Bluenose won the trophy in 1921, 1922, 1931, and 1938.

As a fishing vessel off the Grand Banks, she held the record for the largest catch of fish brought into Lunenburg. Unfortunately, her glory days did not last.

In the 1940s, when sailing schooners could no

A 1929 stamp commemorating the *Bluenose*, a Canadian icon.

longer earn a living against more economic diesel-powered fishing vessels, Walters lost control of the *Bluenose*. She was sold in 1942 to carry freight in Caribbean waters and soon met her demise. On a dark January night in 1946, the *Bluenose* struck a reef near Haiti and was wrecked beyond repair. Fortunately, all hands were saved.

So ended a glorious era of sailing history.

The original *Bluenose* was commemorated on a Canadian fifty-cent stamp in 1929 and since 1937 her likeness has been seen on the Canadian ten-cent coin. In 1955, *Bluenose*, her designer, and her captain were inducted into Canada's Sports Hall of Fame for their achievements in the International Fishermen's Trophy races.

In 1963, the replica ship *Bluenose II* was built in the same Lunenburg shipyard, from the same plans as the *Bluenose*, and by some of the same men. The rigging and sail plan are also identical.

Bluenose II was sold to the government of Nova Scotia for $1 in 1971 by the Oland family of Halifax. In 1994, the province handed possession of the vessel to a group of volunteers that restored the ship to full operational status and maintained and operated her for ten years. The volunteers are known as the Bluenose II Preservation Trust Society, a not-for-profit organization.

Library and Archives Canada, PA-30803

The *Bluenose* was destroyed near Haiti.

Bluenose II is based at Lunenburg and in the summer months visits festivals and events at seaports around Nova Scotia and provides public sailings and charters. She is now operated by the Lunenburg Marine Museum Society.

For more information, contact the Bluenose II Preservation Trust Society in Lunenburg, Nova Scotia, at 1-800-763-1963 or www.bluenose2.ns.ca/.

WORTH NOTING...

Despite their names, the *Bluenose* and the *Bluenose II* are actually black in colour. The origin of the moniker is the subject of much debate. Some say it came from the blue-skinned potatoes the original vessel's crew carried from Nova Scotia to Boston. One story claims the name came from blue dye left on the noses of fishermen wearing homemade woolen mittens.

• • • Oldest Lighthouse: Coastal Beacon

The oldest surviving operational lighthouse in Canada — and in the western hemisphere, for that matter — stands on a granite island about two nautical miles outside the entrance to Halifax Harbour.

Work on the Sambro Island Lighthouse began in 1758; it was lit in 1760 and continues to warn ships of an area of dangerous shoals to this day.

Its first keeper, from 1759 to 1769, was Captain Joseph Rous; its last was J.G. Fairservice, who worked the light as head keeper from 1968 to 1988, when the lighthouse became automated.

The lighthouse tower is built of stone sheathed with wood shingles to protect the mortar from deterioration in the salty coastal atmosphere. Originally white, the tower was given three red stripes in 1908 to make it more visible in snow.

"It has seen vessels of both the Royal and the Canadian Navy pass in peace and war; it has greeted immigrants, war brides, and refugees to a new land; it has watched the passing of the fishing boats, great and small, and the spreading sails of the yachting fleets," says the Nova Scotia Lighthouse Preservation Society. "For sailors, it is the last sight or sound of Halifax, or the first on a safe return."

The original building was of stone and sixty feet high from the base to the weather vane crowning the lantern. The fixed white light was 115 feet above sea level.

In 1906, the tower was heightened to eighty-two feet. At the same time, a first order Fresnel dioptric lens manufactured in France was installed, marking the light as one of Canada's major coastal beacons.

In 1937 Sambro Lighthouse was designated a National Historic Site.

In 1966, the Fresnel lens was replaced with a thirty-six-inch rotating airport beacon that has a range of twenty-four miles and flashes every five seconds. In 1968, the classic iron lantern that crowned the tower was replaced with an aluminum one. The Fresnel lens is displayed at the Maritime Museum of the Atlantic in downtown Halifax.

Over the years, the structure fell into disrepair. Its concrete platform was disintegrating and its protective wooden sheathing was rotting. In 1998 the 240-year-old lighthouse underwent extensive repairs and restoration, and in 2004 careful research established that Sambro Lighthouse is the oldest standing operational lighthouse in both North and South America.

Unfortunately, the lighthouse is not open to the public. For more information, visit the Nova Scotia Lighthouse Preservation Society at www.nslps.com.

WORTH NOTING...

Louisbourg Light, established by the French in 1734, was Canada's first and North America's second lighthouse (the first was the Boston Harbour Light in Massachusetts, built in 1716). During the war between the French and British in 1736, the Louisbourg lighthouse was burned to its foundations. It was rebuilt several times, and the surviving tower, which is not open to the public, was constructed in 1923–24. All that remains of the original structure is the round base of the tower with mortar between the stones. It is located near the existing Louisbourg Lighthouse, on a point of Cape Breton Island across the harbour from the Fortress of Louisbourg, about thirty kilometres from Sydney, Nova Scotia.

AND ANOTHER THING...

In 1900 there were eight hundred staffed light stations in Canada. In 2006, only fifty-two remained, largely because of fiscal cutbacks and the rise of technology on shore and on vessels.

• • • The Original McIntosh Apple Tree: Seeds of a Legend

In the spring of 1811, John McIntosh stumbled upon a handful of apple tree seedlings while clearing a plot of land for the farm he planned to establish in Dundas County.

Instead of tossing the tiny trees onto a pile of brush that would later be burned, he transplanted them to a nearby garden.

By the following year all but one of the trees had died. He nursed it and it slowly grew, eventually producing a red, crisp fruit with a sweet-tart taste.

As early as 1836, McIntosh's son Allan began grafting parts of the tree so that it could be grown in other places by other farmers.

So began the story of the McIntosh apple, which by the 1960s accounted for nearly 40 percent of the Canadian apple market and continues to be the most widely grown and sold Canadian fruit.

Today, more than 3 million McIntosh apple trees flourish throughout North America, all stemming from the single tree discovered by McIntosh.

So, what happened to the original tree?

Unfortunately, an 1894 fire burned down the McIntosh family home and badly damaged the historic tree. Though the family made extensive efforts to nurse the tree back to health, it produced its last crop in 1908 and died two years later.

Photo by Marcus Ray

This monument south of Ottawa sits near where the first McIntosh apple tree was once heavy with fruit.

No one is certain how the tree discovered by McIntosh arrived on his property, but experts speculate that it grew from the seeds of an apple core tossed to the ground by a passerby.

Today, a monument and various plaques mark the spot where the first McIntosh apple tree grew. They're located in the hamlet of Dundela, Ontario, about seventy kilometres south of Ottawa.

• • • Canada's First Newspaper: Old News Is Good News

Since September 2002, a copy of the first edition of the *Halifax Gazette* has been part of Library and Archives Canada's rare books collection in Ottawa.

The debut edition of the newspaper appeared on March 23, 1752, with an editorial by publisher John Bushnell apologizing to subscribers for failing to launch the broadsheet paper on time.

The country's first newspaper was repatriated in 2002 after almost a year of negotiations with the Massachusetts Historical Society.

It's a single sheet newspaper, "yellowed and tattered with age," according to a story in the *Ottawa Citizen*, but still perfectly legible.

The newspaper was purchased for $40,000 and can be viewed online at www.nlc-bnc.ca/halifaxgazette/.

Photo by Janis Ray

Many of Canada's old $1 and $2 bills have been shredded, but some are still held by collectors. (See story at right.)

• • • $1 and $2 Bills: Pre-Loonie/Toonie Currency

In their heyday in 1988, more than 340 million Canadian $1 bills were in circulation. At the end of 1995, nearly 246 million $2 bills were in use.

Since $1 and $2 coins arrived, in 1987 and 1996 respectively, well over half of the $1 and $2 notes once in circulation have gone missing.

In 2006, about 157 million $1 bills and about 110.5 million $2 notes are still out there, says the Bank of Canada in Ottawa. In total, that's nearly 320 million fewer than in the good old days before loonies and toonies arrived.

What happened to all of these bills?

A good majority have been shredded by the Bank of Canada and buried in landfill sites because they were soiled, torn, mutilated, or worn. Others were destroyed by the bank after being returned by financial institutions. Some simply disappeared.

"When the Bank of Canada ceases to issue a denomination, we ask financial institutions to return these notes regardless of their condition. They too are shredded," says Monica Lamoureux, a senior analyst with the Bank of Canada in Ottawa.

The Bank of Canada used to incinerate old bank notes but discontinued the practice because of environmental concerns. And bank notes are not recycled because the process uses aggressive and toxic chemicals to de-ink the paper and reduce it to a pulp, given the durability of the paper and the inks.

Are the remaining notes in people's billfolds? Not likely.

"The $1 and $2 notes remaining in circulation probably aren't used for regular transactions all that often," says Lamoureux. "We expect that a significant number are being held in bank note collections or as mementos, or have been destroyed while in circulation."

The $1 bill was not issued after June 30, 1989. The $2 note ceased being issued on February 16, 1996.

Don't have a $1 or $2 bill in your collection? Samples of the bills can be viewed at the Canadian Currency Museum at 245 Sparks Street in Ottawa (www.currencymuseum.ca) or at most coin shops.

• • • Canada's First Patent: It Measures Up

The first patent issued in Canada after Confederation was registered to William J. Hamilton of Toronto for an invention described as a "machine for measuring liquids."

The patent was dated August 18, 1869. Accompanying drawings dated July 30, 1869, and showing a variety of components, including a piston, guide rod, ratchet wheel, and cylinder, refer to the device as "Hamilton's Eureka Fluid Meter."

Unfortunately the original copy of this patent and twenty-nine others registered after it were either lost or destroyed at some point, says a spokesman for the Canadian Intellectual Property Office (CIPO) in Gatineau, Quebec.

However, copies of all of the original documents related to these patents are kept on microfiche in CIPO's office and can be viewed by the public.

Some of the other original missing patents were for a machine for preventing boiler explosions, a method of making soap, a mustard or ketchup bottle, a hay fork, a machine for coupling railway carriages, and improvements on screw wrenches.

The oldest existing original patent documents since 1867 are for the thirty-first patent, which was issued to a Mr. Bentley of Normanby, Quebec, on September 17, 1869, for "an improvement in locks."

The documents are now held by Library and Archives Canada in Ottawa.

• • • The Tugboat on Canada's $1 Bill: Steamed Its Way to a Museum

Anyone born before the early 1980s will remember the green $1 bill that from 1974 to 1989 depicted a tugboat navigating the log-filled Ottawa River with the Parliament Buildings in the background.

The fourteen-metre-long, fourteen-ton tug was the *Missinaibi*, built in Owen Sound in 1952 by Russel-Hipwell Engines Ltd. and from 1956 owned by Gatineau, Quebec–based Canadian International Paper Company and later the City of Hull (now Gatineau).

The tug made its way onto the back of the $1 bill after the federal government decided to change the design on Canadian paper currency to tighten security and prevent counterfeiting. The Ottawa River photograph, taken in 1963 by Malak Karsh, was one of a number of panoramas to grace the redesigned Canadian paper currency.

Approximately 3.4 million $1 bills were printed between June 3, 1974, when the bill was first issued, and June 30, 1989, when the bill was discontinued. It was replaced in 1987 by the $1 coin known as the loonie.

Today the *Missinaibi* (taken from the Amerindian word meaning "traces left by water") is on display in the outdoor park of the Canadian Children's Museum, which is part of the Canadian Museum of Civilization.

Courtesy of CMC S99-10532, Harry Fosterin

The *Missinaibi* chugged its way onto the $1 bill in 1974 and stayed there until 1989. The original vessel still exists.

REST IN PEACE
• • •
But Where?

NOT ALL THE SUBJECTS IN THIS BOOK lend themselves to an easy interview, and since we don't have psychic powers we had no way of reaching
the many famous Canadians who have died. But we were curious about
where their last resting place is, and we thought you would be too.

• • • Notable Canadians

William Aberhart, who served as premier of Alberta from 1935 until his
death in 1943, was one of the leading proponents of Social Credit govern-

ment in Canada. Known as "Bible
Bill," the popular politician started
out as a schoolteacher and was the
principal at Crescent Heights High
School in Calgary, Alberta, for twenty years. He's buried in Forest Lawn
Cemetery in Burnaby, B.C.

Pierre Berton, who died in 2004,
was one of Canada's best-known
and beloved writers. In addition to
his many books on Canada, Berton
was also a one-time managing editor of *Maclean's Magazine*, a TV
host, and a regular panellist on

Pierre Berton, right, was handy with a
microphone.

CBC's *Front Page Challenge*. Berton was cremated and his ashes scattered in Kleinburg, Ontario, where he had lived for many years.

Charles Best, the co-discoverer of insulin, was born in West Pembroke, Maine, of Canadian parents. In 1921, while studying medicine at the University of Toronto, he met and became the assistant of *Sir Frederick Banting*, who was working on ways to extract insulin. Their work in finding a treatment for diabetes was possibly the most famous Canadian scientific discovery in this country's history. Banting shared half of the credit and monies from his Nobel Prize in physiology and medicine with Best, who died in 1978. He's buried, as is Banting, in Mount Pleasant Cemetery in Toronto.

Tommy Burns, born Noah Brusso in Hanover, Ontario, was the World Heavyweight Boxing Champion from 1906 to 1908 before being defeated by the legendary Jack Johnson. Burns, who died in 1955, was inducted into the Canadian Sports Hall of Fame that same year and into the International Boxing Hall of Fame in 1996. He's buried in Ocean View Cemetery in Burnaby, B.C.

Courtesy of Library and Archives Canada, C-14094

Tommy Burns: one of Canada's finest pugilists.

Best known for the title roles in television's *Perry Mason* and *Ironside*, *Raymond Burr*, a British Columbia native, also acted in more than eighty movies. A long-time Hollywood icon, Burr died in 1993 and is buried in Fraserview Cemetery, New Westminster, B.C.

Known as the father of medicare and most recently chosen the greatest Canadian by CBC viewers, *Tommy Douglas* died in 1986. Originally from Scotland, Douglas came to Canada in 1910 and settled with his family in Saskatchewan. He helped found the Co-operative Commonwealth Federation (CCF) in 1934, which later evolved into the NDP. Douglas is buried in Beechwood Cemetery in Ottawa.

Glenn Gould, whose piano playing brilliance brought him acclaim from around the world, was born in 1932. He made his professional debut just fourteen years later and went on to delight audiences in the U.S., Europe, and the U.S.S.R. He left performing to focus on studio recordings. He died in 1982 and is buried in Mount Pleasant Cemetery in Toronto.

Tim Horton is probably better known today for the donut chain that bears his name than for his prowess as a stellar NHL defenceman. Horton's NHL career began in 1950 and lasted until 1974, when he died in a car crash. He spent most of those years with the Toronto Maple Leafs and also had stints with the New York Rangers, Pittsburgh Penguins, and Buffalo Sabres. But the launch of his famous donut business is perhaps his greatest legacy. Horton is buried in York Cemetery in Toronto.

Yousuf Karsh, distinguished portrait photographer, was a native of Armenia but moved to Ottawa as a teenager. He opened his first studio in the nation's capital in 1932 and became famous for taking photographs of worldwide celebrities and officials, notably Winston Churchill. He died in 2002 and is buried in Notre Dame Cemetery in Ottawa.

His 1957 hit "Swinging Shepherd Blues" brought jazz musician *Moe Koffman* his greatest fame, but he was a fixture in jazz circles for decades, recording music in a range of styles. Koffman died in 2001 and is buried in Pardes Shalom Cemetery in Richmond Hill, Ontario.

Considered one of the greatest Canadian novelists of all time, *Margaret Laurence* was born in Neepawa, Manitoba, in 1926. She studied English in Winnipeg and went on to pen several books that made her reputation, including *The Stone Angel* and *The Diviners*. She died in 1987 and is buried in Riverside Cemetery in Neepawa.

Courtesy of Library and Archives Canada, PA-126393

Lester Pearson.

Marshall McLuhan, influential thinker, professor, and philosopher, gained acclaim in the 1960s with his tome *Understanding Media* and his famous claim that "the medium is the message." Born in 1911, this influential figure wrote several books and received several awards for his work. He died in 1980 and is buried in Holy Cross Catholic Cemetery in Thornhill, Ontario.

CBC television star and fiddler extraordinaire *Don Messer* was born in 1909. His greatest fame came with the TV show *Don Messer's Jubilee*, which featured an array of musicians during its run from the late 1950s through the 1960s. Messer died in 1973 and is buried in Gate of Heaven Cemetery in Lower Sackville, Nova Scotia.

Lester B. Pearson gained fame not only as prime minister of Canada from 1963 to 1967 but also as Canada's only recipient of the Nobel Peace Prize, which he was awarded in 1957 for helping to resolve the Suez Crisis. He died in 1972 and is buried in McClaren Cemetery in Wakefield, Quebec.

Mary Pickford, well-loved silent film star and "America's Sweetheart," was born Gladys Smith in 1892 in Toronto. Pickford started acting as a child and began her film career in 1909. She became the best-known star of the silent era, but also made sound films, winning an Academy Award as Best Actress in 1929. She was a founding member of United Artists, along with her then-husband Douglas Fairbanks. She died in 1979 and is buried in Forest Lawn Memorial Park in Glendale, California.

The man who inspired the formation of the Group of Seven is still revered today for his landscape paintings. *Tom Thomson* is arguably one of Canada's most famous and respected artists. He drowned while canoeing in northern Ontario in 1917, a death still regarded as suspicious by many. Thomson is buried in Leith United Church Cemetery in Leith, Ontario.

Johnny Wayne and *Frank Shuster* were long Canada's most beloved television comedians. The duo performed together for some fifty years, most notably on their many CBC specials and in dozens of appearances on the *Ed Sullivan Show*. Wayne died in 1990, while Shuster passed on in 2002. Both are buried in Holy Blossom Cemetery in Toronto.

Mary Pickford.

Wayne and Shuster.

• • • Canada's War Dead: Gone But Not Forgotten

As many as 117,000 Canadians have sacrificed their lives at war and during peacekeeping missions.

And thanks to such organizations as Veterans Affairs Canada and the Commonwealth War Graves Commission, Canadians know where the vast majority of their fallen citizens are commemorated and can be assured that their gravesites and memorials are well maintained.

The Commonwealth War Graves Commission, whose head office is in the United Kingdom, maintains the graves and memorials of 1.7 million Commonwealth war dead in 150 countries, including 110,000 Canadians who are buried in 75 nations. The Canadian Agency of the Commission, based in Ottawa, cares for Commonwealth graves and memorials in North America.

Approximately 47,500 Canadians are buried in France, 15,800 in Belgium, 12,700 in the United Kingdom, and 5,700 in each of Italy and the Netherlands. More than 19,000 Commonwealth casualties

Robert Parsons, Canadian War Graves Commission

A remote gravesite near Neidpath, Saskatchewan, commemorates Donald Pollock, who died on November 15, 1918. Pollock is buried on his father's farm.

are commemorated in 3,300 sites in Canada in every province and in the Yukon and in all but three U.S. states: Arkansas, Delaware, and Nevada.

In Canada, sites cared for by the commission range from hundreds of well-kept plots in large urban cemeteries such as Toronto Prospect Cemetery, where six hundred victims of the First and Second World Wars are commemorated, to an isolated family plot in a pasture near Neidpath, Saskatchewan, where barbed wire keeps cattle away from the

Courtesy of Veterans Affairs Canada

There are 283 Canadians buried in the Sai Wan War Cemetery in Hong Kong. Another 228 Canadians who have no known grave are commemorated on the Sai Wan Memorial.

grave of Donald Pollock, who died on November 15, 1918, and is buried on his father's farm.

A team of five inspectors visits each grave every five years ensuring that gravestones are cleaned, repaired, and replaced when necessary, says Dominique Boulais, deputy secretary-general for the Canadian Agency, Commonwealth War Graves Commission, Veterans Affairs Canada, which through an agreement with the Commonwealth War Graves Commission cares for the graves of 267 Canadians who died in the Boer War and are buried in South Africa. Most of the 516 Canadians who died in the Korean War are buried in a military cemetery in Busan, Korea, which is tended by the United Nations.

The plots of about two hundred Canadians who enlisted with other countries and died between the Second World War and the Korean War and later are found in various countries and are looked after by Veterans Affairs Canada and Canada's Department of National Defence.

Veterans Affairs Canada strives to inspect each of the graves under its jurisdiction every four years, says Phil Michael, director, National and International Memorials, Canada Remembers Division, Veterans Affairs Canada.

The Canadian Virtual War Memorial, a website set up by Veterans Affairs Canada, contains a registry of information about the graves and memorials of more than 116,000 Canadians who served valiantly and gave their lives for their country. It is found at www.virtualmemorial.gc.ca.

SELECTED
BIBLIOGRAPHY
• • •

Arbique, Louise, and Marc Blais. *Mont Tremblant: Following the Dream.* Mont Tremblant, QC: Mont Tremblant Resort Association, 1998.

Batten, Jack, ed. *Canada at the Olympics: The First Hundred Years: 1896–1996.* Toronto: Infact, 1996.

Bell, John, ed. *Canuck Comics.* Montreal: Matrix Books, 1986.

Boulton, Marsha. *The Just a Minute Omnibus.* Toronto: McArthur & Company, 2000.

Bryden, Wendy. *Canada at the Olympic Winter Games: The Official Sports History and Record Book.* Edmonton: Hurtig, c1987.

Collard, Edgar Andrew. *Montreal Yesterdays.* Toronto: Longmans Canada, c1962.

Cosentino, Frank. *Canadian Football: The Grey Cup Years.* Toronto: The Musson Book Company Limited, 1969.

Cosentino, Frank, and Glynn Leyshon. *Winter Gold: Canada's Winners in the Winter Olympic Games.* Toronto: Fitzhenry & Whiteside, 1987.

Einarson, John. *Neil Young: Don't Be Denied — The Canadian Years.* Kingston: Quarry Press, 1992.

Griggs, Tim, and Lori Horton. *In Loving Memory: A Tribute to Tim Horton.* Toronto: ECW Press, 1997.

Haigh, Kenneth Richardson. *Cableships and Submarine Cables.* London, UK: Adlard Coles Ltd., 1968.

Hall, Ron. *The Chum Chart Book.* Etobicoke, ON: Stardust Productions, 1984.

Hustak, Alan. *Titanic: The Canadian Story.* Montreal: Vehicule Press, 1998.

Lavalée, Omer. *Van Horne's Road: An Illustrated Account of the Construction and First Years of Operation of the Canadian Pacific Transcontinental Railway.* Mississauga, ON: Railfare Enterprises Limited, 1974.

MacDonald, Larry. *The Bombardier Story.* Toronto: John Wiley & Sons, 2001.

Maginley, Charles D., and Bernard Collin. *The Ships of Canada's Marine Services.* St. Catharines, ON:Vanwell Publishing Limited, 2001.

Marsh, James, H. *The Canadian Encyclopedia, Year 2000 Edition.* Toronto: McClelland & Stewart, 1999.

Melhuish, Martin. *Heart of Gold: 30 Years of Canadian Pop Music.* Toronto: CBC Enterprises, 1983.

Ray, Randy, and Mark Kearney. *Canadian Music Fast Facts: Profiles of Canada's Pop Music Pioneers.* London, ON: Sparky Jefferson Productions, 1991.

Robbins, Li. *Don Messer's Violin: Canada's Fiddle.* Canadian Broadcasting Corporation, 2005.

Shales, Tom, and James Andrew Miller. *Live From New York: An Uncensored History of Saturday Night Live.* Boston, MA: Little, Brown and Company, 2002.

Shortt, Edward. *The Memorable Duel at Perth.* Perth, ON: The Perth Museum, 1970.

INDEX

· · ·

Also by Canada's Trivia Guys

The Great Canadian Trivia Book
Explores the noteworthy, notorious, phenomenal, and outlandish sides of the Great White North.

The Great Canadian Trivia Book 2
Kearney and Ray delve even deeper into Canada's curious characters, storied past, and cultural idiosyncrasies.

The Great Canadian Book of Lists
Chronicles a century of achievements, trends, important and influential people, and events that have shaped this country.

I Know That Name!: The People Behind Canada's Best-Known Brand Names from Elizabeth Arden to Walter Zeller
Full of fun facts, intriguing trivia, and engrossing explorations of more than 100 Canadians who beat the odds to become household names.

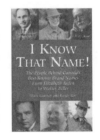

Pucks, Pablum & Pingos: More Fascinating Facts and Quirky Quizzes from Canada's Trivia Guys
A unique collection of trivia bites, quizzes, and graphics that delivers more of the fun, factual fare readers have come to expect from Canada's Trivia Guys.

Available wherever books are sold.
For more information, visit www.dundurn.com
or www.triviaguys.com.